A Combat Reporter's Report

A Combat Reporter's Report

by James B. Sweeney
Lt. Col. USAF (Ret.)

8752

920

SWE

A GROLIER COMPANY

Franklin Watts
New York/London/Toronto/Sydney
1980

Photographs courtesy of

The U.S. Army: opp. title p., pp. 4, 12, 48, 77, 87, 95, and 98; The U.S. Naval Institute: p. 9; The U.S. Navy: p. 16; The Infantry School: p. 58; The National Archives: p. 64; "Chico" Garcia: p. 82.

Library of Congress Cataloging in Publication Data

Sweeney, James B
A combat reporter's report.
Includes index.
SUMMARY: Presents a war correspondent's reports of heroic conduct during times of war.
1. War correspondents—United States—Biography—Juvenile literature. 2. Soldiers—United States—Biography—Juvenile literature. [1. War correspondents. 2. Soldiers] I. Title.
PN4871.S9   070.4'33'0922 [B]   80-13654
ISBN 0-531-04171-9

Contents

Author's Foreword

I

Chapter One
"Baptism by Immersion"

5

Chapter Two
"Yellow Is More Than Just a Color"

17

Chapter Three
"Amen, Amen"

26

Chapter Four
"Not All Luck Is Pure Chance"

38

Chapter Five
"When the Snow Flies"

47

Chapter Six
"To Take the Wrinkles Out"
56

Chapter Seven
"Unsung Hero"
68

Chapter Eight
"Assignment Discovery"
80

Chapter Nine
"The Convert"
92

Chapter Ten
"Farmer in the Dell"
106

Index
117

To
Katherine Roth, M.D.
and
David Roth, M.D.

Author's Foreword

For more than a quarter of a century, it was my chore in the military to listen for, seek out, and report the offbeat human interest story. As a combat reporter, I have been on friendly terms with military leaders, royalty, politicians, church hierarchy, criminals, cops, streetwalkers, waifs, heroes, bums, and many oddities of the human race.

The average person has been endowed with various characteristics, good and bad. Some people have more of one ingredient than another. This is often what separates the useful from the destructive. Hitler, as an example, was obsessed by racial hatred and a lust for power. As a result, he left the world such memorials as Buchenwald and the graves of millions of dead soldiers of various national origin. On the other hand there was Bob Hope, who possessed an urge to bring a laugh to every GI, no matter where that GI's foxhole might be hidden. Regardless of the difference between these two individuals, my task was to report their accomplishments.

Being a combat reporter was a sort of game, a dangerous game. Where some men liked to play golf or tennis, the ardent combat reporter enjoyed doing his bit aboard a submarine, tank, jeep, or fighter plane. The casualties were high—terribly high. According to official Army Signal Corps records, combat reporters suffered proportionately a higher rate of casualties than even the infantry.

At times, unbeknownst to himself, the combat reporter was used as a spy, a bomb evaluator, an implement of psychological warfare, or a criminal investigator. Sometimes his assignment came from on high, sometimes through routine channels, and many times by way of his own imagination. He was shot at, lauded, envied, hated, and even, upon rare occasion, decorated. He was forgotten, remembered, reassigned, and forgotten all over again. His stories were censored, read, vilified, or left to mold in some office in-basket. Seldom, if ever, were they by-lined.

General George C. Marshall, that wonder of wonders, had a great appreciation of the printed word. Unfortunately, he considered combat reporters nothing more than a necessary evil. However, at times he was known to loosen up to the point where he joked over this rare breed of humans.

"There once was a jockey," he told an intimate group meeting on the subject of army combat reporters, "who was able to talk to horses. One day he was scheduled to ride a horse that had never won a race. 'Listen to me,' he told this nag, 'if you lose the race you'll be pulling a milk wagon in the morning.' So the race commenced, and as they came into the homestretch, the horse was last. The jockey took to using his whip unmercifully. Finally the horse could stand it no longer. He turned his head and shouted, 'Hey up there, cut it out. I got to be at work by three o'clock tomorrow morning.' "

The point the general was so aptly making was that you could not beat a serviceable story out of a combat reporter, but, given his head, he never failed to cross the finish line in his own fashion.

The stories recounted in this book are not fictional, nor are they entirely as seen through the eyes of one reporter. Many of the news releases cited never made it up the military chain of command. They are true except for minor changes. In a few instances, names have been changed. This has been done to protect the innocent, to shield the families of the deceased, or to substitute for those names that time has erased from memory.

Whatever pain, joy, misery, or laughter these pages convey, one thing should be kept in mind. Most of the actors who played a part in these bloody theatricals of war are dead. In fact, many never even lived to the final curtain.

Signed,

JAMES B. SWEENEY,
Lt. Col. USAF (Ret.)

*A soldier grieves for his buddy just killed in action,
while a medical corpsman nearby methodically fills out
the dead soldier's casualty tag.*

Chapter One

"Baptism by Immersion"

World War II jungle warfare was a crucible. It took the most timid of army draftees and turned them into killers. The change was not a pleasant one, nor was it usually accomplished easily.

As an illustration, at dawn a frightened youth would be dumped on a bullet-infested beach that quickly became strewn with the blood of his closest buddies. He moved forward only because of loudmouthed noncoms who appeared to be without fear. He dug a hole for himself, was routed out, bellycrawled, and fired a rifle aimlessly until his supply of ammo was exhausted. Then he dug another hole for himself, ate what he could out of a tin can, and settled down to survive the hellish experience of his first night in the jungle.

Private Daniel Darling was different from nine million other men of arms. He was a combat reporter. In place of a .30 caliber M-1 rifle, he packed a .45 automatic handgun and a notebook—all of which had come about through a series of events that had begun in high school. There, an English teacher had impressed upon his mind a belief that the pen is mightier than the sword. As a consequence, he managed to graduate from college with a degree in journalism. But shortly thereafter, Uncle Sam sent him a draft notice. It began with the corny expression "Greetings." So it was that he had to leave town.

From that point on, Darling had struggled, in the best of raw-recruit fashion, to do nothing more than remain inconspicuous, stay away from the eagle eye of any drill sergeant, and simply be "What's-his-name in the rear rank."

Unfortunately, Private Darling was tall and his army serial number was A1111111. This easy-to-remember combination made him readily recognizable on a roster. As a result, Darling, Daniel (no middle initial), Private A1111111, caught every stinking detail passing through the malicious mind of a first sergeant. At least so it seemed to Darling. He cleaned toilets, emptied garbage, washed dishes, proved himself inept on the rifle range, and was sent back to latrine detail. He stood guard, marched in parades, exhausted himself on kitchen police, and shoveled coal with which to keep the furnace aglow in the officer's club.

And that is how Darling got his big break.

In passing through the clubhouse early one morning, he noticed a bulletin board. From it hung a lone piece of paper held in place by a thumbtack, and on the paper were scribbled several names. Darling, having time to waste, paused to indulge his curiosity. Did the names represent a work detail? No! To his surprise, the paper was an official notice that read:

```
ATTENTION! School for combat reporters. Of-
ficers needed. Must have journalism back-
ground. Assignment requires strong experi-
ence in news reporting, editorial writing,
broadcast news, documentary film scripting,
and/or photography. Those qualified, write
name, rank, and serial number below.
```

There were only three names on the list, none of which Darling recognized. Looking around and seeing no one, he scribbled, *"Darling, Daniel, A1111111, New York Times, two summers as a police reporter."*

He omitted any mention of rank.

Two weeks later he was surprised to be handed a set of orders. Daniel Darling, A1111111, was to proceed to the Infantry School, Fort Benning, Georgia, as a student for the newly created class of combat reporters.

At first, Darling was delighted. But his delight soon wore off. Shortly after he reported to the school, he was enrolled in several painfully sophomoric journalism classes—as well as some backbreaking classes in running obstacle courses. He was not alone in his misery. There were others in the class, four others, in fact: Stein, Herman, A192838; Murphy, Patrick, A824960; Olcheskie, Howard, A561098; and Van Vlack, Jan, A128633.

Van Vlack, the oldest among them, seemed to enjoy the misery. When they suffered, he exulted. When they found a moment of ease, he recited depressing facts. Following one miserable afternoon of push-ups, knee bends, and cross-country jogging, he said, "You guys hear about the kill ratio?"

"Kill ratio?" Darling asked. "What do you mean?"

"The kill ratio among army combat reporters is higher than in the infantry," Van Vlack said, gloating. "Not one in ten survive the first year. Our chances of living through this war are practically zero."

"You're talking about our death rate, that right?" Olcheskie asked. The thought of death was especially distasteful to him. He had a wife and son back in Rochester, New York.

Van Vlack nodded, but before he could say anything more, a drill sergeant called them to attention. "The following men have volunteered for immediate combat duty: Private Darling, Private Stein, and Private Murphy."

A roar of protest went up from the three. "We didn't volunteer for anything," they shouted in unison.

The sergeant put his fists on his hips and thrust his jaw forward. "When I says yez have volunteered, yez have volunteered."

Which is how it happened that Private Darling found himself in the Pacific making a beachhead landing with a million or so other guys who had one thing in common. They all suffered from dragging feet and a racing heart. It was fear at its worst. But they hung in there, clawing, battling, and spilling guts over each yard of contested ground.

It wasn't until things quieted down and the beachhead was established, that Darling remembered to file his first combat report. It went like this:

Dateline: Somewhere in the Pacific--Night fighting is hell. Cringing in darkness, a Yank dares not fire a gun. The flash is certain to betray his location to enemy troops creeping through the entwined vegetation. These night crawlers are a plague that comes with darkness. They're little men, stripped naked, a short-bladed bayonet between their teeth. Adept at slipping through the inky entanglement, they literally feel their way over the ground. Whenever they locate a foxhole, they slide in and strike with the speed of a cobra.

Rookies can hear them out there daring anyone to squeeze off a shot. "Amelican pig soldier, him too scare for fight," these crawling animals yell into the darkness. A soldier fool enough to answer would be tracked down and killed. Worse yet, the enemy tries to capture a Yank, stake him out on a flat patch of ground, and begin the soul-shattering process of skinning him alive. The screams

*A World War II beachhead landing on one of the
Solomon Islands in the South Pacific. Overhead,
a barrage balloon observes the action.*

```
and agonized cries of the wounded bring res-
cuers charging through the night, only to be
cut down with machine gun fire.
    By the time the sun comes up and killing
can be resumed in a more orderly fashion,
a rookie, if he survives that first night,
is on his way to becoming a combat infantry-
man adept at dealing out death. End of news
release.
```

Darling sent off his release via a sympathetic radio operator. The promptness of an acknowledgment amazed him. Upon numerous occasions he had found it necessary to contact higher headquarters concerning mistakes in pay, travel allowances, or overdue leave. Replies were seldom forthcoming. Things were generally left to unravel themselves. However, in the case of his first dispatch, a complaint came through in prompt order.

```
To Darling, Daniel, A111111l. This message
in two parts. Part one: News release re-
ceived. Unacceptable at this level. Primary
object of combat reporting is to relay in-
formation considered useful in support of
home front morale. Horror stories not deemed
within said category. Heroic actions of
uniformed forces needed. Human anecdotes
stressing courage on part of individual sol-
dier desired. Part two: Remember basic ten-
ets stressed in special training school and
adhere thereto. End of message.
```

The last part of the message jarred Darling. He recalled the unofficial credo of the school: "A story a day keeps reassignment away." It was the thought of reassignment that shook him. Reassignment meant being tossed back to garbage detail, cleaning toilets, or training to be a dogface in some infantry outfit. He grabbed paper and pencil and commenced to write.

<u>Battle</u> <u>of</u> <u>Leyte,</u> <u>Pacific</u> <u>Theater</u> <u>of</u> <u>War</u>--
This tropical island has been occupied by
Japanese troops for over two years. Enemy
soldiers are tough and by now well entrenched. Three days ago Americans hit them
with the battle-seasoned 7th Infantry Division, out of California, and the not-so-
battle-hardened 96th Division from Oregon.
That's how the two Grimes brothers, Harry
and Joe, met for the first time in three
years.

Harry was a tough, battlewise sergeant in
the 7th and had earned his stripes helping
defeat the Japanese at Attu, Kiska, and
Kwajalein. Joe was a replacement in the 96th
and had yet to fire a shot in anger. They met
during a beachhead landing that chopped the
two divisions to pieces and scrambled what
was left into a single unit. It wasn't much
of a reunion. The Japanese laid into one
sector with knee-mortars and swept what was
left standing with explosive bullets. Two
men dived for a vacated foxhole and there
they were--Harry, the older by two years,
full of anger and hatred for the enemy, and
Joe, the novice, scared. They threw their
arms around each other and stayed low. Joe
cried a little, for he was on the verge of
panic.

A dirty-faced lieutenant crawled to the
lip of their foxhole. He saw them laughing.
That made him curse and yell for them to get
out of there. He wanted to flank what appeared to be a 77-mm mountain gun the Japanese had set up in a pillbox. Harry dragged
Joe along with him and told him to stay close.
As they crept along with a lot of other guys
the lieutenant had mustered, the enemy commenced to bring up foot soldiers in support
of the gun position. A section of 81-mm mortars, dug in back at the American OP [opera-

*Infantrymen soon learn to
"hug the ground" during enemy fire.*

tions post], opened up and gave the Yanks support. The platoon force, under the lieutenant, got close to the pillbox before they realized the enemy gun was a dual purpose, rapid-fire anti-aircraft cannon. So they threw grenades, waved up some B.A.R. [Browning automatic rifle] men, and peppered the emplacement with small-arms fire.

There was no time to be wasted. The lieutenant called for a charge. The men of the 7th and 96th moved in fast while the enemy was still pinned down. They flanked the bunker, knocked the gun out with grenades, and turned to meet a banzai charge. The battle deteriorated into a wrestling match, the Americans killing two for every man the enemy laid low.

Then the battle was over, and each force dragged back prisoners for questioning. Harry, satisfied with his performance and happy to be alive, turned to see how Joe had fared. There was no Joe. The younger brother was missing. The wounded hadn't been moved as yet, so Harry checked them out. His brother wasn't among the lot. Fearing the worst, he went about the battlefield and rolled over each of the dead; no Joe. It wasn't until darkness closed in that he figured out what had happened to his kid brother. The night air was filled with screams of a Yank who was being tortured. Without a doubt, the pain-wracked voice was that of Joe.

Harry knew the score. He crawled around until he found his first sergeant, a rough guy by the name of Doyle. He asked the sergeant for permission to lead a patrol in an attempt to rescue his brother. Doyle referred him to a Lieutenant Baker, who said, "Heck no!" Then he explained to Harry that such rescue attempts were suicide; orders had come down that no more were to be launched. "Get back to your place in the line, Sergeant. Keep your men alert for a night attack."

Harry returned to his troops. Later, when Sergeant Doyle came to check on how things were going with the men positioned along the perimeter, he realized Harry Grimes was missing. He went looking for him. There was no Harry Grimes. The first sergeant reported this to Lieutenant Baker, who got mad at having his orders disobeyed. "If I find he went out there to rescue his brother, I'll court-marshal him," he told Doyle. "So you let me know the instant he returns."

Moments after this conversation, both noticed that the tortured man's screams were suddenly cut short. "Well," the lieutenant said, "Grimes must have reached his brother."

"Yeah," the first sergeant agreed, glad that the ghastly screaming had stopped. "You still want to see him if he gets back?"

"Absolutely. He disobeyed orders. I'll have his stripes for that."

The rest of the night was relatively quiet. A few star shells, a couple of creepers caught in the act, and a hand grenade or two. Morning was a different story. With the first ray of light the Japanese attacked in force. They were met with a wall of gunfire. Then the 7th and 96th counterattacked. The American forces steamrollered the enemy. Harry was there, fighting as hard as ever. He only grunted when the first sergeant told him to see the lieutenant as soon as the action let up.

The fire fight progressed yard by bloody yard. The Yanks gained some, lost a little, and finally broke through to take a hundred yards. It was then Sergeant Doyle sought out Lieutenant Baker and said, "Sir, have a look at what I found. It presents a problem."

The two moved forward till they came to the body of an American who had been staked out and hacked into pieces. He was surrounded by three dead Japanese. "That's Grimes' kid brother," the sergeant said. "And look at what killed him."

There was a bayonet sticking out of Joe Grimes' chest. Both men knelt and examined the handle. "That's an American bayonet," the lieutenant finally said, knowing the implications his words carried.

"Yeah," the first sergeant agreed. "Harry must have killed his brother to end the suffering."

"And that," stated Lieutenant Baker in a positive voice, "is willful murder."

The two remained stooped over the body for several minutes. It was raining now, and moisture made things twice as miserable. Finally the lieutenant cleared his throat, mumbled a little, then got out what was on his mind. "If I ever get captured like this, I hope some friend will do as much for me."

"Me too," intoned Doyle. "That Harry guy should get a medal; he sure showed a lot of guts."

Lieutenant Baker nodded. "Not a bad idea, Sergeant. See about writing him up for a Silver Star, or at least a Bronze Star."

Sergeant Doyle won't have to do that. Today Harry Grimes was killed in action.

End of news release.

There followed no complaints from higher headquarters. The story was accepted without change.

*This "daisy chain" is passing food supplies,
medicines, and ammunition to soldiers on the beach.*

Chapter Two

"Yellow Is More Than Just a Color"

They say it takes one to know one. That is why the instant combat reporter Jan Van Vlack met Major George Edgewood, an MP (military police) officer of the 82nd Airborne Division, he knew him for what he was—nasty and hard-nosed. The two men were in complete harmony. They got along fine.

The port of Salerno was the dumping ground for men and supplies needed to fight the war in Italy. Ship after ship lined up to take a turn at off-loading. Troops, tanks, trucks, jeeps, food, medical supplies, clothing, and weapons were funneled through makeshift facilities. There was no such thing as accountability, just massive heaps of merchandise destined for the battlefront.

The local Mafia was having a heyday—hence the presence of Major Edgewood. He had been sent to stem black-market activities by cutting down on stolen supplies. He was to sniff out the leader of the gang and destroy the gang's activities by arresting its members. Private Van Vlack sensed a story in the major. That's how they became friends. One night the reporter sought out the officer and asked him directly, "Sir, you've been here eight days. Have you detected the gang leader as yet?"

Major Edgewood had the mean-eyed features of a hawk about to strike. "Yeah, sure. Now I'm preparing to administer the death penalty."

"Death penalty?" Jan gasped. "I thought you came here as a police officer, not a judge advocate!"

"Right, my boy, but if I put the collar on this creep, he'll get himself shipped back to the States. There he'll hire a lawyer. In short order, the case will be squashed for lack of evidence."

"He's an American?" Jan asked with surprise.

"Correct. Tony Teresa's a Chicago gangster. He managed to get himself sent over here as a civilian adviser to the military. He's supposed to be an expert in freight handling. Which is like sending a fox to guard the henhouse. In nothing flat, this jerk's organized local thieves into running everything from murder to hijacking."

"But killing this Teresa hood will only get you in trouble. It could stand as a murder rap against you. What about your military career?"

Major Edgewood grinned with the look of a lion licking its chops. "Me kill a man? Toosh! What a horrible thought. Why shucks, me and Tony have already become buddies. We play blackjack together."

"You mean you'd gamble with a crook like that?"

Again that savage grin. "Yeah, sure. And better yet, he cheats at cards and I'm a real pigeon. An easy mark. Already he and his cronies are into me for eight hundred bucks."

Van Vlack whistled. "That's a lot of money."

"Not really," the major said. "It isn't much when you know your opponent's weakness."

"His weakness?"

Major Edgewood chuckled. "He's loudmouthed, a braggart, and yellow. A neat combination. With qualities like those I can put a rope around his neck."

The major got to his feet. He took a .38 six-shot revolver out of a shoulder holster. With loving care he flipped the weapon open and inspected its contents. The cylinder held only five shells. The firing pin rested on an empty chamber. This was wise. If the gun were to be dropped or jarred, it would not discharge accidentally. Snapping the weapon shut, he holstered it and said, "Join me, Private Van Vlack. You can come along as my jeep driver. That way you'll be witness to the action. Give you a fine perspective for a story."

They went out to a jeep that was cranked up and ready to go. The two rode in silence. It was dark. They were permitted to use only blackout lights. These were nothing more than tiny slits of purple light. Driving required the utmost attention. The narrow streets were jammed with marching troops, supply vehicles, and scurrying civilians. Major Edgewood seemed to give directions more by instinct than by eyesight. At last they parked by what appeared to be a shell-torn farmhouse. They walked to the rear and knocked on a planked door.

After several moments, a rusty bolt slid free. The door opened a crack. A voice growled, *"Si?"*

"Tony Teresa," Edgewood said, "I want to see Tony."

The door opened a bit more. *"Prego, prego,"* the voice said.

They entered, but it was too dark inside to see. The voice resumed. "You will pleased to follow me."

They pushed through a blackout curtain, went down a flight of rickety steps, and stood in a small cellar. The room was lighted by the harsh glare of a field lantern. Three men sat at a wooden table. The man who ushered them in resumed his seat to make it a foursome. They were a scraggly lot, except for one. He, obviously, was an American, a loudmouthed American. Jumping to his feet he roared, "Welcome, welcome, my friend Edgewood. Come in. Have a seat. Join me and my neighbors in a bit of cards."

It was evident the game was for money. Dollar bills, Italian lire, and French francs littered the table. Before Edgewood could answer, the American rushed over, grabbed Jan Van Vlack's hand, and began to pump it. "Come in, my boy. Welcome. Any friend of the major is a friend of mine. Like to play cards, huh? Like to gamble a little, right? Well, here the—"

"Knock it off, Tony," Edgewood snapped. "He's my driver. Just invited him in out of the night air."

Tony appeared disappointed, but he recovered quickly enough. Throwing an arm around the major, he roared, "Hey! You know these guys. They is Jake-the-Bear, Bloody Joe, and Ripper. Nice boys. Here, have some wine. Let's play cards, yes?"

Jan found a seat in one corner of the tiny room. What a bunch of bandits. Everyone packed a handgun. They were American guns, too. Except for Tony Teresa, the others were dressed in rough clothes. Tony wore an expensive plaid suit, a diamond stickpin on a blazing green tie, and a chunky gold ring on one finger. The automatic gun he carried in a shoulder holster had pearl handles. "Hey you," he yelled at the man indicated as Ripper. "Get the major some fresh wine."

Teresa, waving a deck of cards, then turned to Edgewood. "Hey, Major. We'll play blackjack. Ah man, that's my game. Good ol' twenty-one. Can't beat it."

He began to shuffle the deck in a stilted way. Then he dealt awkwardly. It was clear the man was a cheat, and not a good one at that. He slipped cards off the bottom and used a crooked shuffle. No one protested.

The Ripper returned with a jug, which was passed

around to the accompaniment of Tony Teresa's loud mouth. "Ho, you guys all afraid to buck up against me, huh? Scared to put up some real money, right? So it ain't like back in Chicago when I played for maybe two or three thousand bucks on the turn of a card. Like one time I caught Trigger Mike Colicci cheating. So I gunned him down. He falls dead onto the table.

"Which is what I'm telling you. Don't let me catch nobody playing this here game crooked. Twenty-one is *my* game, and there ain't nobody better."

Major Edgewood banged his cards to the table. "That's the trouble. It's *your* game. You can't play but one game. You're afraid to play any other kind of game."

Shocked silence filled the room. The boss of bosses had just been called scared. They all waited, each man tense as a coiled spring. No one could call Tony Teresa afraid and be left to live. Tony leaned forward and snarled, "How you mean that, soldier?"

Edgewood leaned forward. They came almost nose to nose.

"Like I said, Tony," Edgewood answered, "you're scared to play any kind of game but blackjack, which is a child's game. For a real man's game, you ain't got the guts."

Tony was breathing deep. He was conscious of the others around him. If he let the major call him yellow and get away with it, his empire would collapse. "You got a game in mind?"

"Yeah," Edgewood said. "My kind of game. But it takes money to play and it takes guts. You ain't got either."

Teresa didn't know when to keep his mouth shut. "You name it, punk. I can outplay you at any game you got in mind."

Edgewood sat back. "Double or nothing what I owe now."

"You owe a thousand bucks, punk. You lose on this and you owe me two thousand bucks, dead or alive."

Edgewood nodded. "Now let me explain a little something about my game. We cut cards to see who plays first. The one who goes first has only one real chance of winning. The second man has it all in his favor."

Tony reared back. "What kind of game you got in mind?"

Edgewood gave that grin of his, looked at the others, then came back to Tony. "What's the matter, Tony, you yellow?"

Again the verbal slap. Tony was stung. It showed in his face. His eyebrows lowered, his teeth bared, and the olive tone of his skin turned red. He licked his lips and swallowed before daring to speak. "And we cut to see who goes first?"

Major Edgewood nodded. His eyes were as cold as Arctic ice. "Yes. You want to cut?"

Tony began to unwind. He recognized a good thing when he saw it. He picked up the deck of cards and commenced to use that awkward shuffle of his. Everyone but Major Edgewood could see a card being palmed. Even Jan Van Vlack was drawn to the table. He stood behind Tony Teresa and watched. He wanted to yell *stop* to the major, to tell him he was a fool to bet on the turn of Teresa's card. Something warned him to keep his mouth shut.

Tony was relaxed again. It showed in his mouth. He started to run off at the lip again. "Okay, wiseguy. So we cut the cards to see who goes first, or second."

"Right," the major agreed.

"So low card goes first, high card second."

To this Major Edgewood agreed with a nod.

"Okay, soldier," said Teresa. "Now what's your game? Tell us about it."

"Roulette," Major Edgewood said in a calm voice.

Teresa looked confused. "Roulette? We ain't got no wheel, you dummy."

Major Edgewood said, "Ah, but we do."

Teresa looked around the table. "Listen to this dummy. If we got a roulette wheel, I don't see none. What kind of roulette you playing?"

Slowly, ever so slowly, Edgewood withdrew his .38 revolver and laid it in the center of the table. "Russian roulette, my friend. The gun holds one empty chamber. You spin the cylinder, then place the gun to your head and pull the trigger. With luck, you hit on that single empty chamber."

Teresa turned white. Sweat appeared on his forehead. "Th-That ain't no game."

Edgewood looked to the other men at the table. They were hunched forward, eager for the showdown. Silently each nodded approval. Then the major reached out, swung open the cylinder, and exposed five bullets. He looked at Tony, amused. "I believe you're yellow, Teresa."

The gangster's dilemma was obvious. If he got up and left, his own thugs would kill him in revolt. Then he seemed to remember something. He grinned. "So we cut to see who goes first?"

"That's correct."

Jan Van Vlack was tense. He found himself gripping his automatic. Yet he offered no protest when Tony Teresa shuffled the deck, laid it beside the revolver, and said, "Cut."

Major Edgewood appeared to be growing shaky. He hesitated. "Cut," Teresa snarled. "You want to play rough. Okay, so now you cut."

The major reached out. Gingerly his fingers sought a place in the deck. He made his cut. The card that showed was the jack of hearts. Not too bad. It could be a winner. Tony Teresa picked up the deck, gave it a fake shuffle, put it down, and cut. He turned up the ace of spades.

"Hah, you dummy. Now go ahead and play your game of Russian roulette."

All eyes were on Major Edgewood. There was no backing down. He wanted to play rough. Okay, here it was. His game. His rules.

Reaching out, the major snapped the cylinder shut. His hand shook as he picked up the gun.

"Wait!"

That was Tony Teresa's voice. "I don't want no cheating, see. You let me spin that cylinder."

"No," the Ripper snarled. "Me spin. Me do twirling."

The other gangsters at the table nodded. The major held the gun while the Ripper reached over and twirled the cylinder with his thumb. Then, almost mournfully, he said, "Now you go."

The major's hand was quivering as he raised the muzzle of the weapon. He placed it against his right temple. His eyes were wide with fear. He licked his lips and hesitated.

"Go ahead, dummy," Teresa snarled.

Major Edgewood's finger tightened on the trigger. As the pressure increased, the hammer drew back. Everyone waited, breathless, tense. Here was a man about to kill himself. The hammer was all the way back.

Click!

No explosion. Nothing but a hollow click. He had hit the empty chamber. As if he were about to faint, the major weakly laid the revolver on the table. Then he shoved it toward Teresa. "Your turn."

Teresa's face showed an absence of blood. His eyes bulged. He licked his lips. "I . . . ah . . ."

The Ripper leaned forward, as did Jake-the-Bear. "You take turn now, so I make like a spin for you," the Ripper said. The cylinder clicked as it was twirled about.

Tony Teresa was quivering with fear. Eyes on the gun, he appeared unable to make himself move. His head began to shake. "N-No," he finally managed to whisper. "No, I ain't going to do it."

With that, his hand jerked toward the pearl-handled automatic in his shoulder holster, but not quick enough. Van Vlack had his .45 against the back of Teresa's head. "Freeze," he said. Reaching around, he pulled Teresa's gun free and threw it to the floor.

Tony stared helplessly around the table. All eyes showed contempt. Big Mouth had turned out to be a coward. Yellow. He got to his feet slowly, then spun around and dashed for the stairs. The other gangsters followed in wild pursuit. Soon only Major Edgewood and Jan Van Vlack were left in the room.

"Wow!" the reporter said. "You sure played that close."

Major Edgewood reached for his gun. He flipped open the cylinder and ejected the five shells. Then he took another five bullets out of a pocket and began to thrust each into a chamber. Confusion showed on Van Vlack's face. He reached over and picked up one of the ejected bullets. It was light as a feather. Much too light. He was amazed. "They . . . they're—"

"Dummies," the major said laughing. "The whole bunch of them are dummies."

And maybe he wasn't just talking about bullets.

Chapter Three

"Amen, Amen"

Captain Wells Faulkner was steaming mad, as could easily be seen by his angry pacing up and down the tiny field office of Colonel Howard Nord. Yes, he was a doctor and he knew when someone was faking an injury. "That Corporal Emir Abdel does *not* have a bad back. He's a fraud."

Nord, commanding officer of the 115th Infantry Division's field hospital, was also a doctor. After six months of splicing together the bodies of half-dead combat casualties, he, too, was weary of the European campaign. He understood what it was that was irritating this captain. Too many soldiers faking combat fatigue. Even General George Patton himself was raising a ruckus about that. "Get those fakers out of hospitals. Get 'em back to duty."

But it wasn't that easy. A conscientious medical man couldn't go amidst the beds pointing a finger every which way and saying, "You, out! You're a fraud, a fake. Get going —back to the mud, filth, and slime of killing."

To spot the true fraud took a bit of study. Some of the fakers were good actors, as seemed to be the case with Corporal Abdel. He was either suffering from a very painful back or staging a very effective play.

There was a third man in the room. He was seated beside Colonel Nord's makeshift field desk. "Meet Lieutenant Hunter," Colonel Nord said. "He's with the CID [Criminal Investigation Division]. He has something to tell us about this case."

That quieted the medical captain. He said, "Hello," and pulled a folding chair over to the desk. He didn't like these undercover spooks. Nobody could tell who the devil they were or what they were up to. "Hope it's worth listening to, for a change."

The remark was uncalled for. The investigative officer was trying to be cordial. Unshaven, dressed in mud-caked combat clothes, he hadn't taken a shower in a week. The whole of France was a war zone. Having to constantly travel in a jeep wasn't exactly what you would call fun. These hospital types were holed up in a permanent building. They could get cleaned up once in a while. For a moment, his face flushed with anger, but he managed to control his temper. Taking a folder out of a briefcase, he laid it on the desk. "Here are results of an investigation pertaining to one Corporal Emir Abdel, 115th Infantry."

"That's our man," Captain Faulkner agreed. "I filed that complaint over three months ago."

"Right. We've had a tail on that soldier ever since. He does nothing wrong. Everything's by the book."

Colonel Nord waved a hand in protest. He was new to this command. The last CO (commanding officer) had taken a piece of shrapnel through the head. German bombers were not that careful about where blockbusters fell. Churches, hospitals, combat troops—all were the same to them. "Suppose one or the other of you fills me in on this patient."

"Darn right," Faulkner said. It was obvious he had a

gripe about this case. "Three months ago, I'm in charge of a combat medical detachment. A jeep runs over a mine. Boom! It gets blown apart and three men along with it. This Corporal Abdel is brought in as a litter case. He's got no more than a cut on one cheek. So I slap a little medication on his face and mark him *duty*."

"Was he riding on the jeep?" Nord asked.

"No. This jerk is in a column marching along the side of the road. Percussion knocked him flat."

Nord studied Captain Faulkner. "So, Doctor, what made you call in the CID?"

"This guy won't go back to combat duty. Says he can't. Claims his back has been injured."

"Why didn't you send him to the rear. Get rid of him?"

"No," Faulkner growled. "No way. This guy is a fake. It's my word against his. I intend to see this slob goes back to duty . . . combat duty."

Nord nodded. "So you kept him at the aid station until you were transferred here. Then you brought him along. That correct?"

"Yes sir," the medical captain answered. "Which is when I contacted the CID."

Colonel Nord turned to Lieutenant Hunter. There was a questioning look in his eyes. The investigative officer caught the signal. He started talking. "On receipt of the captain's complaint, I put a good man to watching this Corporal Abdel. Three of my best men were casualties in your hospital, so I had plenty of backup."

"What did they observe?"

"That Abdel never once walked in an upright position. He used a cane. Constantly complained of pain. In the shower, the mess hall, the latrine, wherever, he never straightened his back."

Nord thought about these facts. "What's this guy after?"

"Medical discharge. Wants one hundred percent disability," Lieutenant Hunter answered. "He makes no bones about it. One of my men is buddy-buddy with him. They've been living together, relaxing together, walking together. Still, this Corporal Abdel claims he can't straighten his back. We have no reason not to believe him."

"I'll give you a reason," the captain snapped. "X rays show there is nothing structurally wrong, so I pump him full of medication. Nothing makes him relax."

"How do you know his claims are not valid?"

Faulkner leaned forward. "I gave him heavy sedation. When he was asleep, I straightened him out. He never seemed to be aware of his position until fully awake. Then, zap! He goes from proper position to full bend. No in-between. No gradual tightening of the muscles. Just zap. There he was. All bent over and grabbing for that cane of his."

Nord found himself intrigued by the story. "You checked out his military records, Lieutenant?"

"Yes. Nothing there to be suspicious about. Native of Colorado. He's of Arabian ancestry. Has a high school education. Was drafted."

"Nothing suspicious?"

Hunter gave a grunt. "Nothing suspicious; maybe something curious."

Nord didn't like roundabout talk. "What do you mean by *curious?*"

"Well," the lieutenant said slowly. It was as if he'd already given the matter deep thought. "This guy is recorded as being a devout Muslim. Now, since he's been in the hands of the medics, he's become a convert."

"To what?"

"Catholicism. My undercover man tells me he's become a very religious person. Visits Chaplain Collins regularly for religious instruction. Attends mass almost daily."

"That *is* curious."

Hunter nodded. "For a devout Muslim to suddenly become a devout Catholic. Yes, I'd say very curious."

Nord thought about this. "Talked to the padre?"

"No," the lieutenant admitted. "This being a medical case, well, ah, I thought you—"

"Hogwash," the colonel growed. Lifting his head, he bellowed, "Orderly!"

Almost instantly, a soldier appeared. He had on a white armband emblazoned with a red cross. His helmet showed the same marking. "Sir?"

"Find Chaplain Collins. Tell him I'd like to see him."

Turning to the lieutenant, Nord asked. "Anything else?"

"One other thing." Lieutenant Hunter sighed. He was a tired young man. "Got a cup of good ol' American coffee?"

In short order three mugs of very strong brew were set before them. For a time, they sat in silence, sipping. A rough-looking major came in. "What the dickens you want now, Colonel, permanent absolution? That'd allow you to—"

Then he saw the lieutenant, a stranger. His tone became more formal. "Oh, ah, ahem. I'm Father Collins, beloved chaplain to this bunch of sinful medics."

They all laughed. It was obvious this sharp-eyed clergyman was joking. Hunter noted this. Not the kind of guy a man could easily pull a con job on.

"Say, Padre," Nord said. "You got a guy by the name of Corporal Abdel under your wing. What sort of a fellow is he?"

"A fake," Collins replied at once.

"How so?"

"Says he wants to become a Catholic, but he's absent-minded about the whole caper. Sometimes he's with it; more often not. He doesn't even get to praying when the bombs fall close. That's a sign my teachings aren't getting through to him."

Outside, there was the rattle of machine guns and the roar of a light prop-driven aircraft in low flight. Both Colonel Nord and Captain Faulkner glanced at their watches. "Ten after five," Faulkner said.

"Yeah," Nord agreed. "That's Bed-Check Charlie, right on schedule."

"Bed-Check Charlie?" Lieutenant Hunter asked.

"A Nazi aircraft," the colonel explained. "It does a low-level strafe job every evening about sundown. That's when most men are off guard, a little too relaxed. He slips through one of the mountain passes. Radar can't detect him. Makes a run over villages like Vic, Lourdes, or Saint Gaudens."

The padre was edging toward the door. "That all?"

The colonel nodded. "Thanks, Chaplain. Be seeing you."

"And now the bad news," Lieutenant Hunter said with a halfhearted laugh. "We can't continue this investigation any longer. Not enough manpower. Too many more important investigations."

Faulkner was on his feet with a roar. "This guy is a fraud. He'll get out on a medical, which means that you and I will be paying for his support the rest of our lives."

"No," the lieutenant interjected. "I've a solution."

Nord waved the captain to his seat. "Tell us about it, Lieutenant."

"Well sir, there's this guy I know. He's a captain like myself. His name's Sweeney. Has a group of combat reporters. Some of his men are good investigators. They can sometimes crack a case faster than we can."

Both Nord and Faulkner were silent. The suggestion wasn't quite acceptable. Still, it had some appeal. "So you're suggesting this friend try his hand on Corporal Abdel?"

"Not he himself. One of his men. He's got an ace combat reporter named Stein. Doesn't have much rank—he's only a private first class. None of those reporter types get many promotions. But he's good."

"Stein. That's a Jewish name. Why him?" Nord asked.

"I'm not sure of the particulars. However, I've been given to understand that Private Stein was religious editor on a large daily newspaper. Knows a good deal about different religions."

Faulkner was frowning. "How's he going to be brought into the hospital, as an orderly or what?"

Hunter got to his feet. He returned the folder to his briefcase. "As a patient."

"What kind of a patient?"

"Battle fatigue. Same as Corporal Abdel. That should start them off as buddies."

Lieutenant Hunter was about to leave. He appeared to have an afterthought. "One thing you should know. If Stein cracks this case, it goes public. These combat reporters aren't undercover agents. They're newspaper reporters."

Nord agreed with a nod of his head. "That's what we'd like: to publicize this battle fatigue fakery; make sure people back in the States don't lionize these jerks."

"We understand each other," Lieutenant Hunter said. He shook hands, saluted, and left.

Four days later, a patient named Stein was admitted to the hospital. His folder didn't reveal much. Private first class, first name Herman, antitank gunner, 3rd Infantry Division, 7th Army. In going through the admission files, Captain Faulkner noted the name. Could this be *his* Stein? He went looking for the man. After a bit, he found a likely patient and instantly knew him to be the right man. He was sitting on the edge of a cot playing cards with Corporal Emir Abdel.

"You're Stein?" the captain asked gruffly.

"Uh-huh," the man acknowledged. He didn't show much respect. A hospital bathrobe indicated he was a patient.

"What's your problem, Stein?"

Immediately the patient went into an act. "Ohhhh my back, Doc. It's killing me. I can't do nothing. Just pain all the time. It's something terrible. Why I can't hardly move and—"

"Be in my office within thirty minutes. I'll examine you then."

The doctor hesitated for a second. He was on the verge of asking Abdel how he felt. The slender, black-haired man was bent over in an awkward position. A cane lay by his side. There was a look of hate on his cunning features. Without comment, the doctor turned and walked away.

A half-hour later, Stein limped into Faulkner's examining room. He closed the door, and the two abruptly relaxed. "So you're *the* Stein, huh?"

Private First Class Herman Stein smiled. "Well, Doc, I'm the Stein that just signed up to undergo religious instruction. I'm about to become a Roman Catholic."

"You, a Catholic? What's the angle?"

Stein was young, vigorous, and alert. "I don't know yet. This guy Abdel has some sort of a religious gimmick going for himself. It's some kind of an out. He won't tell me what it is but hints I can work the same deal."

There was a sharp rap on the door. Major Collins stuck his head in. "Ah, caught you two conspirators in the act."

Faulkner laughed. "Come in, Padre. I understand the religious conversion business is booming."

"Yeah," the chaplain said. He drew up a chair and flopped down on it. "I'm thinking of letting out franchises."

After the laugh, he turned serious. "Bad news. The army's got to release this Abdel. Either ship him Stateside for clearance or release him here in France."

Faulkner took the information like a smack in the face. "He's a fake, a fraud. We'd be aiding and abetting a crime."

Major Collins shrugged. "Too many patients at lower levels. The chief of chaplains is pressing to get medical cases home or discharged over here."

"Wow!" Stein gasped. "That's playing right into Abdel's hands. He's hot for a discharge in France."

"Why?" Faulkner asked.

"Can't even guess. Although he was moaning and groaning about not having any wheels to get around on."

Captain Faulkner was pacing the room. He was upset. "Imagine, a sneak like this Abdel making a fool out of the medical profession. I don't like it."

Chaplain Collins was more practical. "You drive, son?"

"Yes sir," Stein replied.

"Good. Upon occasion my jeep is free. See if you can put it to good use. This guy Abdel can't drive in his bent-over condition. So you play big brother. Meantime, I've got to be putting discharge papers through for him."

It was an unhappy trio that broke up. A mere corporal had outsmarted all of them. Emir Abdel had made a monkey out of Uncle Sam. "Just one thing," Chaplain Collins said to Stein. "Keep me informed."

Three days later, Stein called Collins. "Chaplain, hospital administration just handed Abdel his discharge papers. He's free as a bird."

"Yeah, a vulture," the chaplain grumped. "What a sin. To be handed a one hundred percent disability discharge based on fraud."

"And one other thing. This guy Abdel asked me to drive him across the mountains this afternoon. Said he wants to go to some little town or other. I didn't catch the name. It looks like he might be getting ready to reveal a sort of gimmick."

"He still bent over?"

"Sure is, Chaplain. Furthermore, he's as nervous as all get-out. Hospital authorities gave him a lecture. Said if it could ever be proven his claim was based on fraud, they'd prosecute."

"Which means that he will have to spend the rest of his life bent over."

"Right, Chaplain. Anybody spots him walking upright and he's on his way to a federal prison."

"Stein, you drive Abdel wherever he wants to go. But keep in close touch. You can always get through to me on a field phone. Incoming hospital calls get top priority."

"Okay, Chaplain, will do."

It was early evening before Herman Stein could get back to Chaplain Collins on a field telephone. "Major," he asked, "are you sitting down?"

"No, why?"

"You better be when I tell you what happened."

"Quit the jokes, Stein. Give it to me straight."

"Okay, Padre. You're familiar with the famous Roman Catholic church at—"

Bed-Check Charlie roared overhead. Machine guns clattered, bullets ricocheted, and glass splintered. For a moment or two the noise was deafening. Then the enemy was gone.

"Go ahead," Chaplain Collins said.

"That famous place called the Basilica of the Rosary?"

"You mean you're in the city of Lourdes?"

"Yeah, exactly. It's the place where all those miracles have taken place over the years."

Chaplain Collins was getting a sick feeling in his stomach. "Yes, go on."

"Well, now they got a new miracle. The miraculous recovery of Corporal Emir Abdel. He visited that church today and suddenly he's cured."

Chaplain Collins was almost overwhelmed with disgust. "You mean, Abdel not only made a mockery of his country, he also made a mockery of God?"

"Correct. He's out in the street, loaded on wine, and dancing around like a monkey."

"And there's nothing we can do about it?"

"Nothing at all, Major. A miracle's a miracle. No one would dare censor the ways of the Lord."

Fury shook Major Collins. "May God punish that Abdel for such evil."

Stein made no reply. He seemed to understand the chaplain's frustration. After a moment or two, the chaplain regained control of himself. "Thank you for the news, Private Stein. And be careful of yourself. Bed-Check Charlie was last seen heading in your direction."

Chaplain Collins hung up and dropped heavily into a chair. How could he bring himself to report such evil to Colonel Nord and Captain Faulkner. They'd take it badly. Bowing his head, he began to pray. He asked the Lord to forgive the corporal for the terrible mockery he had committed. To falsify a miracle was the act of an anti-Christ. A heathen. The chapel at Lourdes had been the source of cure for hundreds of people—true miracles. Now this horrible mockery. Thirty minutes later he was still praying when the phone rang. He caught it on the third ring. "Chaplain's office. Major Collins speaking."

"Herman Stein again, Chaplain."

"Yes," Chaplain Collins acknowledged. "What now?"

"You asked that the Lord punish Corporal Abdel for his mockery of God and country, right?"

Chaplain Collins was taken aback. "Well, ah, yes. An expression only. I meant no malice."

"Well He did, Major."

"Who did what, Stein?"

"The Lord. He punished Corporal Abdel. He's deader than a mackerel. Half the top of his skull got knocked off."

"Wh . . . What happened?"

"Bed-Check Charlie made one pass alongside that church of yours. Abdel caught a ricochet bullet off the side of the building."

There was a pause. Then the chaplain pronounced his eulogy: "Amen."

Private Herman Stein could see no harm in lending his voice to a prayer of this nature. Softly, before hanging up, he too said, "Amen."

Chapter Four

"Not All Luck Is Pure Chance"

Don't look for it on any map; you won't find it. Khorram is an oasis located on the shores of the Persian Gulf. The inhabitants are mean-tempered, the camels spit at you, and the flies are so vicious they draw blood with every bite. Heat, sand, and brackish water are the area's outstanding characteristics. Overlayered across it all is the combined smell of unwashed bodies, animal dung, open sewers, and strewn garbage.

"So it's a living," Private Willie Hawke would say as he dealt the cards. "I seen worse in Brooklyn."

Willie had been a professional gambler and soldier in the U.S. Army for seventeen years. In the course of that time he had experienced some good luck and some bad luck. Being assigned to Detachment E, 378th Port Battalion, wasn't what he deemed the best of luck. For Khorram was that unit's base of operation. It was here that German prisoners were brought from around the Middle East before being shipped to a regular prisoner of war center.

The fact there were prisoners streaming through the area made life bearable, for prisoners had war medals, watches, rings, and personal mementos that could be bought cheap. In turn, these would be converted into cash at the gaming table. Transient American troops loved to send such trinkets home to their wives or girlfriends. But Willie would use a Nazi *Luftwaffe* pilot's badge, for instance, that cost him two American dollars, to buy five dollars worth of poker credit. As a result, Willie the gambler was making hundreds of dollars every month—which was nothing new for him. A rumor occasionally surfaced that Private Willie Hawke was a millionaire. Although Willie denied all such talk, he knew it to be true.

Captain Harold Schmidt was Willie's immediate superior. Schmidt was from Milwaukee, spoke fluent German, and interrogated prisoners. Since Willie also spoke German, as well as French, Yiddish, and Hungarian, the captain kept him close at hand.

"Willie," the captain would threaten, "someday I'm going to have you promoted to sergeant."

The threat would make Willie turn pale. Promotions endangered his livelihood. As a private, he could comfortably gamble amidst any group of enlisted men. Corporals and sergeants were inclined to belittle him. A soldier who couldn't make a few stripes in seventeen years must be awfully stupid. It cost them money to learn that Willie was anything but stupid.

Besides, it was corporals and sergeants Willie had to con into buying Nazi medals, shoulder boards, collar patches, and insignia of rank. Men with stripes were men with money. Such gentry loved to show superiority by haggling a stupid private out of gold buttons from a *Luftwaffe* general's uniform for four dollars, when any fool knew they were worth twice that in the States. What they didn't know was that Willie bought whole sets of buttons from hungry Germans for fifty cents. He believed in quick turnover. Take your profit, triple it at the poker table, and send it to roost at Chase Manhattan Bank.

Khorram had but one permanent building. It was what remained of an abandoned French Foreign Legion outpost. The building consisted of two large rooms, between which was a door. Willie's duty station was inside the room farthest from the front entrance. There, Captain Schmidt had set up a field table and a couple of chairs, nothing more. It was a depressing place, lighted only by whatever happened to come through either of two narrow windows. Sometimes it was sunshine, quite often sand, and always bugs carried in on stifling breezes.

Private Willie Hawke stood at one end of the table. He wore a helmet liner on which was lettered GUARD. A web belt held a long nightstick. He stood, listened, and glowered at what each prisoner had to say. *Oberlieutenants* were sullen young men; they gave only name, rank, and serial number. It didn't matter. They had little information of note. On the other hand, general officers liked to shoot off their lip, maybe out of some sort of guilt complex. They had been captured. Therefore, as tacticians, they were less smart than Americans. This hurt. Hitler's supermen not as brilliant as slovenly Yankees? Nonsense. To salve wounded pride, they explained the unfortunate twist of fate that led to their being taken prisoner. The more they talked, the more Captain Schmidt learned about enemy troop movements. Shortly thereafter, such information was radioed to Allied commanders.

Captain Schmidt and Willie had worked out a routine. On signal, Willie would pull open the door and yell, "Next man." A guard in the outer room would shove a prisoner forward. If it was an officer of upper rank, Willie would give a snappy salute, beckon him to the single folding chair, close the door, then come and stand by the captain.

Should the prisoner show pride, smugness, and Nazi aloofness, the two Americans knew they had a pigeon. Verbal barbs were thrown. "Too bad, *mein Commandant,* that *der Führer* did not give you proper training in military tactics."

Or perhaps an opening gambit might be, "You *Luftwaffe* generals are well uniformed. What a shame you were not taught to fight."

Instant reaction. Wounded pride. The Nazi officer would become arrogant, loudmouthed, and a braggart. To have a mere captain talk to him in such a fashion was insulting. Meantime, as he shot off his mouth, Willie was appraising the man's uniform.

Occasionally a tough nut would fall into their hands. If this happened and the Nazi officer wanted to fight, Willie would unlimber his club. With this weapon, the boy from Brooklyn was an expert. He could raise lumps, bruise, or knock flat the hardest head in the German Army—all within the twinkle of an eye.

Corporal Patrick Murphy, A824960, stumbled upon Private Willie Hawke one evening. As a transient combat reporter, Murphy was free to interview whomever he wished. He found himself wishing he hadn't chosen Private Hawke. The first ten minutes cost him eight dollars for Nazi trinkets; the second ten minutes cost him twelve dollars for bucking Willie at cards. After that they became friends. Willie let up on the pressure.

It was through Willie that Corporal Murphy met Captain Schmidt, and following that meeting Murphy was invited to sit in on an interrogation session. The procedure promised to be interesting. At first, it was. Then it became routine, followed shortly by boring. Willie would open the door and yell, "Next." A prisoner would be escorted to the camp chair, following which there were questions, answers, arguments. The prisoner would eventually be escorted out the door and another brought in.

Then through the door strutted *Generaloberst* Hans Forster, commander of a *Fliegerkorps*—young, proud, bitter, and full of patriotic venom. A fighter pilot, he had been shot down while leading a flight over Al Hajara. He stomped into the room, ignored Willie, and came to a halt before Captain Schmidt's desk. Clicking his heels, he raised his right arm and bellowed, *"Heil Hitler."*

The shout angered Willie; he unlimbered his nightstick.

Captain Schmidt was intently studying a folder containing records compiled on *Herr* Forster. He never looked up. "Private Hawke, teach the general courtesy."

It was like the strike of a snake. Willie's club swung and neatly peeled the German's uniform cap off his head. It went flying across the room. The Nazi general spun about, fists clenched and teeth bared in a snarl, ready to charge. But something stayed his anger. It was Willie at the ready. The wiry Yank with the big club looked formidable. Captain Schmidt glanced up from the folder.

"What a shame you couldn't have displayed a little of that fight while aloft, *mein General.*"

Forster pivoted to face the captain. "You Yankee dolts. You fools. I demand respect. Under the rules of war—"

Willie's club thumped the general between his shoulder blades. "Stand at attention!"

Again the general pivoted, fists cocked. He was at the boiling point. Still, something held him back. There was the look of the killer in Willie's eyes, the look of a man without compassion.

Captain Schmidt seemed unmindful of the byplay taking place between these two. "Are you a pilot, *Herr General*?"

This was an insult. General Forster's chest was covered with winged insignia of the *Luftwaffe*. Even his lapel insignia carried the markings of a fighter pilot. "Fool, scum of an American, what do you think these medalions are for?"

"Political accomplishments, no doubt!"

General Forster looked as though he was about to explode. "You Yankee dolts. *Mein Staffel* hass shot down no less than one hundred fifty-two Allied bandits and . . ."

Abruptly the general gained control of himself. A crafty look crossed his face. These swine. They were *trying* to anger him. "Hah, such stupid pigs. You are unfit for a reply."

"Say, General," Willie drawled. "Tell you what, I'll give you a dollar American for that there tin cross what you got on a ribbon."

The general turned beet red. "You idiot. That is the Prussian Iron Cross. It is Hitler's highest personal award."

"Er, gosh," Willie said in an apologetic voice, "I sure didn't know that. Tell you what—I'll make that a buck-fifty."

"Now, about instructions afforded German flying cadets," Captain Schmidt continued, "do they teach you anything about aerial tactics?"

General Forster ground his teeth. Carefully selecting each word, he said, "Big, brave Americans. You know how to harass a downed pilot. Two against one. Like mad dogs badgering a proud stag. You can only snap at my heels."

"For the moment that seems to be adequate," the captain said. His voice showed just a touch of boredom. It was a further irritant. "Now, *mein herr,* why was it you showed such inflight stupidity?"

The general hunched forward, as if he were about to lunge at the captain. Instead, he snarled. "Stupid, you say? Why you two Yankees illustrate what ignorance exists in the Allied forces."

"Ohhhh?" the captain questioned. After all, this is what he wanted—an argument. To get this Nazi talking. "Tell us about it."

Forster straightened up. Standing erect, he thrust out his

jaw. "I am a general because I can outthink stupid underlings such as yourselves."

Captain Schmidt was amused. Was the general now playing the same game that he and Private Hawke played? Interesting. "Come, General, don't continue to act the Nazi fool."

"Ha, you dunce. Yes you, Captain. You could not qualify to be a noncommissioned officer in *der Führer*'s military establishment."

Now it was Captain Schmidt's turn to grow angry, a fact that did not escape the general's attention. "Yes," he shouted, "you! A dunce, a dummy, a lunkhead, a buffoon!"

The captain was on his feet. He was taller than the general and showed more muscle. "And you, General, like Hitler, are all mouth. No affirmative action. Just mistakes, blunders, stupidity. Murder the weak, overpower the defenseless."

Willie the gambler stood between the two angry officers. He remained icy cool.

Forster again thrust his jaw forward. "Ha, stupid Yankee, you say, 'overpower the defenseless.' Yet you have this numbskull standing by with a club. If I do not do as you wish, he beats me on the head. It is you, pig of a Yankee, who is overbearing, arrogant, domineering."

Schmidt was angry. The tables had been turned on him. He seemed to have lost control of the situation. "You're all mouth, General. Shut up while you still have teeth to talk through."

General Forster was rigid with contempt. "Ha, Yankee swine, you and your idiot assistant with a long club. Such a dolt. He could not hit me on the head with that stick if I stood but one foot in front of him."

Now it was Willie who reacted. He stepped dangerously close. "Say that again."

General Forster turned as though expecting some such reaction. "You heard me, thick head. I can stand face to face with you and make it impossible for you to hit me on the head with your stick."

Both Private Willie Hawke and Captain Schmidt were intrigued. What kind of foolishness was this? This Nazi general had something in mind. He wanted to play a game of wits, to show that he could outthink two Americans. Willie was the first to respond. "If I hear what you're saying, General, you have the power to make my club useless against your will to control physical force?"

"Right!" Forster snapped.

"And the stakes? What sort of a bet is involved?" Willie asked.

The Nazi officer thought about this. "Hmmm," he finally said. "If I lose, you may have my medals."

"And if you win?"

The general gave a nasty laugh. "In front of all your troops, in front of all the prisoners of war, you two must kneel and kiss my feet."

Willie's eyes were asparkle. He looked at the badges, unit patches, and insignia that covered the general's chest. What a treasure! Greed took over. Still, a little caution remained. "We stand inches away from each other, face to face. If I hit you on the head, I win. If I can't touch you, I lose."

"More positive," General Forster said. Reaching over, he picked up the file folder Captain Schmidt had been reading. "I shall stand with my foot touching one end of this folder, you with your foot touching the other end. Yet you will be powerless to hit me."

"That's a deal."

General Forster was quick to act. He walked across the room, dropped the file folder to the floor, and pulled the door shut—with himself on the other side. Half the folder lay exposed beneath the door. Then the general's voice came through the thick planking. "Okay, you American dolts, I'm standing on my end of the folder. Now hit me with your club."

Both Captain Schmidt and Private Hawke were trapped. Willie's big mouth had gotten them into trouble.

"Come, come, you American dolts, do not keep your superior waiting. Either hit me or comply with the agreement."

Captain Schmidt was furious. He turned on Willie with a vengeance. "Fool! See what you've gotten me into? I'll have you court-martialed, given a dishonorable discharge!"

Willie was thinking. He had to find a solution quickly. His cold, calculating mind spun at a great rate.

"Hit me, Yankee idiots, or kiss my feet," Forster's voice again came through the door. "But do not keep me waiting."

Willie's face lit up in a smile.

"What's so funny?" Captain Schmidt yelled.

Willie raised the club overhead. With the swiftness of a tiger he whipped open the door, leaped onto the folder, and brought the club down in a vicious swing. General Forster was caught offguard. He tried to fall away from the blow. Not quick enough. His body thunked to the floor and remained there.

Private Willie Hawke knelt and began to strip the badges off the general's chest. "The idiot," he said. "He didn't mention anything about not being allowed to open the door."

Corporal Patrick Murphy nudged Captain Schmidt aside. "Man, oh, man, what a story! I got to get me to a typewriter. This should get Willie Hawke his sergeant stripes."

Private Hawke tried to stop him. The combat reporter was gone. He shrugged. "Ah well," he said out loud, "some I lose."

Chapter Five

"When the Snow Flies"

Major General Hans Laske was a soldier utterly without compassion. To say that he was ruthless would be to pay him a compliment. The Marquis de Sade, the granddaddy of all cruelty, would probably have been sickened over the methods used by this German *Wehrmacht* soldier. Nevertheless, such a characteristic assured Laske of two things: a place of favor on the staff of Adolf Hitler, and wealth.

As commandant of the German Central Supply District, with headquarters in the mountain village of Troueville, Hans Laske made French people in the area cough up more than seven hundred thousand francs in cash, plus a man-sized casket full of jewels—a feat he accomplished within six months, two weeks, and four days.

At that time, Hans Laske had never heard of the Thunderbird Infantry Division. It was a National Guard outfit made up of units from Oklahoma, Colorado, New Mexico, and Arizona. By the time these tough foot soldiers had joined in the drive across France, their division had collected a staggering total of 3,021 awards and decorations. Furthermore,

Tanks lend support to foot soldiers
on a drive across enemy territory.

they possessed the distinction of having amongst their ranks Private Daniel Darling, combat reporter *extraordinaire*.

However, these were facts about which Major General Hans Laske knew nothing and cared not at all. True, the Allied landing on the Cherbourg Peninsula was taking hold. And true, too, that Charles de Gaulle, that French upstart, with the help of Americans was organizing underground forces. This was causing some unrest, especially in the little town of Troueville. But Hitler had recently perfected pilotless planes. These he loaded with explosives, to be jet-propelled toward British cities. Such a fine instrument of war, Laske felt, would soon cause the Allies to back away from France. And Laske could cope with the unrest in Troueville. After all, he was a military man, a man who had fought his way up from the ranks.

It was the severe winters and the French kids Laske couldn't cope with. He liked neither. In fact, he hated both. The children were noisy, and the winds of early fall were freezing. Be darned if they weren't already sub-zero. At least they felt that cold. So, as he went about his duties, he bundled himself in warm clothes, constantly fortified himself with good French wines, and used his riding crop to slash at whatever children got underfoot.

Then came the snow. The wind quit, and in its place came white flakes. For a time they drifted down leisurely. The ground was cold, so the flakes did not melt. They just lay there, like the advance element of a battalion onslaught. It was as if they were waiting for support forces to catch up. And catch up they did. More and more flakes drifted down out of the skies.

"*Herr General*," an orderly said as he knocked discreetly on the door to Laske's office, "word has been received that your wife and son will arrive from Berlin within the hour."

Hans Laske almost had a heart seizure. At a time like

this, his fat Bavarian wife was bringing their brat of a son to Troueville? Things must be bad in Berlin.

"*Gott in Himmel,*" he thundered. "Get the women out of the house. Throw away the empty *schnaps* bottles. Clean up a couple of rooms."

The general was always fending off visits from Hilda, his overendowed wife. Their ten-year-old son was forever wanting to see how important Daddy was amidst the subjugated people of France. Now here they were. And it had to be snowing. Regardless, he must put on a show. He must demonstrate what a strong-willed ruler a true Nazi could be in an alien land.

No need for worry. His son put on the show. The day following his arrival, the boy walked the crooked little streets of the quaint village and punched the nose of every French kid he came across. His father, and the armed guard that accompanied them, thought this hilarious. His mother smiled and allowed as how the apple had not fallen far from the tree. On the second day of their visit, the boy borrowed his father's riding crop. Equipped with this and a powerful-looking armed guard, father and son went looking for more children to beat up on. However, word had gotten around. Whenever the general and his son appeared, French youngsters disappeared.

That was how Laske and son came across the snowmen. The weather had cleared, and as the pair walked the streets, they heard childish laughter. They tracked it down and found that French children had been building snowmen on the front lawn of the village school. Now the scene was abandoned. The children had been given a signal; all had scampered indoors.

The general's son was fascinated. He walked amidst the round-bellied figures, scrutinizing each with a critical eye. Some were quite good. One wore an old hat, cocked over chunky eyes made of chipped rock; it had a piece of stick for a nose. Another, resembling a woman, had a skirt of newspapers and hair from branches of a tree. The boy was entranced.

"Papa," he said, "I want some children to play with, to build snowmen with."

General Laske was glad to hear this. He was tired of escorting his son about. Besides, his mind was troubled by other matters. The war news was not good. It appeared as though the Allied invasion was meeting with some success. Swine! They would be defeated. *Der Führer* would see to that. Still, the way Allied bombers were sweeping across France, almost at will. . . .

"Papa," the boy had to scream a second time. His father appeared to be lost in thought. "I want children to play with."

"Ah, *ja, ja,*" the general said, as if snapping out of a trance. Turning to a sergeant, he waved his riding crop at the school. "Turn out the children. Have them build snowmen for my son."

General Hans Laske then did a foolish thing. Leaving his personal bodyguard—the sergeant—and four troopers with his son, he strolled across the street to a café. After all, he did have a holstered automatic pistol as a personal sidearm, so he had nothing to fear. These Frenchmen had long ago been subjugated. Later, the sergeant, who was busy directing the building of snowmen by a large group of sullen children, recalled seeing the general come out of the café.

But that was the last any German ever saw of Major General Hans Laske. Blip! He disappeared.

"And then where did he go?" A staff colonel roared at the sergeant.

"I cannot say; the last I saw of him, he was walking down the street."

But you were supposed to remain with him at all times."

"*Nein.* He gave me orders to stay with his son."

"And after a bit, you returned here with his son?"

"*Ja, mein Colonel.* The boy is with his mother."

The colonel was furious. He hated the bitter cold as much as he hated the general. Still, things were going bad for the *Wehrmacht.* The general was needed. "Turn out the garrison. I want this town searched. It has only been about five hours since the man disappeared. There must be some trace of him to be found. I want to know what has happened."

Troopers stormed up and down the streets. They forced their way into homes, into wine cellars, cafés, and hotels. It was snowing again, this time heavier than before, so they had to look among the snowdrifts. They even went to the little village school and searched it from top to bottom. The children were still outside building snowmen. Now that the general's son was no longer with them, they were laughing happily. The troopers scattered the kids, told them to get on home.

The soldiers searched, but the mystery remained. What had become of the general?

Hitler, on hearing of the mysterious disappearance of Major General Hans Laske, sent a team of his sharpest detectives to Troueville. They went through the village minutely. Nothing. Not so much as a trace.

That winter was especially bad for the Nazis. Everything was going wrong. Syria joined the United Nations, and Egypt approved a declaration of war against the Axis. Finland declared war on Germany. Storm troopers began to desert. Troueville saw its first advance elements of the Thunderbird Division.

At first, the people of the village were frightened. These grimy, bewhiskered Americans came charging across the snow. They weren't pretty to look upon. But they were tough; they could fight. The Nazis discovered this and fled. Then the villagers turned out to welcome the hordes of Yanks that thundered into the village. Freedom! It was in the air.

People began to be themselves again. Captain Levittre,

Commandant du Police, put on his forgotten uniform and became active in civic matters. Old Man Glemot, who had lost a leg in World War I, took to wearing his Legion of Honor on the threadbare rag that served as an overcoat. Ancient Father Piquet donned his hidden cassock and publicly announced that Sunday masses would again be held in what was left of the village church.

It was from these people, all too old to go off to war, that Private Daniel Darling first heard of the strange disappearance of Major General Hans Laske. The weather had turned warmish and these good folks, along with others of their kind, had gathered on streetcorners to bid the battle-weary Yanks welcome. They pointed out collaborators, hidden ammunition dumps, likely booby traps, and told of Nazis in hiding. On several occasions, people remarked about the strange disappearance of a German general. It was mentioned as though the matter were the town's private little joke. Darling's journalistic ears pricked up.

Darling began to ask questions but was simply shunted about. Always, at mention of the matter, he got nothing more than a grin, a shrug, or a wink.

Finally, out of compassion, Old Man Le Boutillier, the barkeeper in a local café, suggested that he take the matter to Father Piquet. If the padre wished to reveal the truth to the press, why that would be satisfactory with the rest of the townspeople. So Darling set out to find the reverend. Locating him was not easy, however. Father Piquet, who could now openly visit his sick or wounded parishioners, was on the move. But Darling was persistent. He trod through the gumbo-like mud that coated the streets. He looked under dripping eaves and inside shattered buildings. Still no Father Piquet.

Then, quite abruptly, he came upon the old priest hurrying along the main street. His cassock was a dead giveaway. Darling stepped in front of the aged clergyman and said in his best high school French, *"Pardon monsieur,* may I speak with you?"

The priest stopped and replied in almost perfect English, "What is it you wish to say?"

"I've been told you know the secret of the Nazi general who mysteriously disappeared in your town."

The priest clamped his jaws tight, as if he were preparing to shake his head and say no. Then he looked about and seemed to note the melting snow. He watched as a large icicle dropped from an overhanging roof. Spring was coming. He smiled. "Yes, my son, I will tell you the story. But we must walk even as we talk, for many of the sick await my visit."

The two set off, winding a precarious way between speeding personnel carriers, motorcycle couriers, jeeps, tanks, and supply trucks. As the two stepped along, the priest described Hans Laske's terrible cruelties. He had tortured, maimed, and killed many of the villagers. Everyone despised the man. They also feared him, for he was a drunk and subject to unpredictable rages. "Nevertheless, we whispered amongst ourselves about how best he could be done away with."

"You, too, Father?" Darling asked with some surprise.

"Me above all others," the priest said. "And why not? Upon occasion I have been called upon to exorcise a devil. Why not rid our village of Lucifer himself? It could be worse."

"And so you villagers murdered the general?"

"The general drank himself to death."

"And how was that accomplished?"

"White arsenic in red wine cannot be seen nor tasted. He simply got hold of a bad bottle of wine."

"So he was poisoned. But what became of his body?"

They had reached the little schoolhouse. Children no longer played in the yard. Their melting snowmen had turned the ground into a quagmire. They could be heard laughing and romping about indoors.

The wrinkled old priest held his arms apart in a gesture that encompassed the entire school. "There, my boy, you have your answer."

"You mean, inside the building? Perhaps in the cellar?"

"No, no," said the padre. "Nothing so elementary, nothing so crude. His rotting carcass would have stunk out a signal to the Nazis. And they were looking for him; believe me, they were looking for him. We had to have someplace more ingenious, someplace completely insulated."

"And that was?"

Father Piquet turned and solemnly shook hands with Private Darling. "I must leave you now, for I should not be present when you discover the body. The sight of the dead man would bring glee to my heart. That, I believe, would be sinful."

Before Darling could utter a word of protest, the man and his cassock had disappeared between columns of marching soldiers. Turning his attention back to the school, Darling commenced to wonder. The gentle warmth of the sun was causing ice atop the roof to flake away and slide with a crash to the ground. The snowmen, built with such childish glee, were now askew. Some had even fallen apart, a head here, a round belly there. It was then the realization hit Private Darling like a sledgehammer.

"God a'mighty," he gasped as he slogged through the slush to the only snowman that still stood upright. It was heavily coated with ice. Slowly, very slowly, he reached up to the head and slid his fingers under the crust of ice. When he pulled, a sizable portion broke loose.

"Christ," he yelled as he leaped back. For there, less than an arm's length away, was the perfectly preserved body of Major General Hans Laske. And the orbs of the eyes, black and frozen hard, were glaring at him.

Chapter Six

"To Take the Wrinkles Out"

Death was something Staff Sergeant Brian Shirer had to reckon with on a daily basis. He was a mess sergeant, which meant that he always had to have food ready for every fighting man's stomach, and this on a twenty-four-hour basis. No let up. Patrols went out morning, noon, and night. Sundays, Mondays, or holidays, the troops took to the field. Not all came back. Those who did were hungry, cold, and haunted by the violence they had witnessed.

In calculating how much meat and potatoes it would take to feed a platoon, the sergeant would have to take into account the kill ratio. No use wasting valuable food. If, for instance, Sergeant Elliott was leading a patrol, food allotments could be cut by as much as twenty-five percent. Elliott was a reckless devil from Texas. He took a lot more chances than most patrol leaders. On the other hand, Sergeant Zaphire was a cautious leader. His losses never ran more than ten percent. Regardless of who was leading what patrol, Brian Shirer steadfastly met their demands: hot coffee, warm soup, thick slices of bread, nourishing vegetables—anytime, anyplace, under any conditions. If you were hungry, the sergeant had a morsel that would, as he put it, "take the wrinkles out of your belly."

To accomplish this was one devilish chore. Especially for a man of fifty-five, which is how old Sergeant Shirer happened to be when Corporal Howard Olcheskie met him. At the time, Olcheskie was hungry, not for food but for a story. He was a combat reporter. Worse yet, he was a combat reporter who hadn't filed a story in a week. Headquarters wouldn't like that.

Olcheskie saw Brian Shirer for the first time while the mess sergeant was standing knee-deep in mud, turning out pans of fresh-baked spice cake. Impossible? Not for Shirer. Let bullets fly and mortar shells thump against nearby hills. A night patrol was due back at any moment. By gosh, those boys would have spice cake and fresh-brewed coffee along with their regular breakfast—provided, of course, they came back alive.

Sergeant Shirer was short, dumpy, and pale of face. There was about him a great sadness. His eyes showed it, as did the droop of his mouth. He seldom smiled. When he first joined the outfit in North Africa, or perhaps it was Sicily— nobody could remember for sure—he seemed to have a mission in life: to find his two sons lost in combat.

"They were sent out on a scouting mission," a platoon sergeant told Olcheskie. "They didn't come back."

Combat records were nonexistent at squad level. Replacements arrived, were shoved into the swirl of combat, and came back limping, on a litter, or in a body bag. Then more replacements. There was no paperwork. That was rear-echelon stuff. Out here, gunfire was all that mattered.

In the beginning, Old Man Shirer made a pest of himself, constantly asking, "You hear anything about a sergeant named Tommie Shirer? Or maybe a private named Joe Shirer?"

The answer was always, "Who? Never heard of 'em." No wonder. The squad, platoon, and company to which the broth-

Infantrymen wounded in combat are treated by emergency medical personnel and then sent on to a field hospital.

ers once belonged had been wiped out several times over. After a while, Pop Shirer, as the troops got to calling him, ceased asking. He became withdrawn and even more dogged in his attempts to feed hungry soldiers.

Olcheskie would have discovered a number of startling facts had he checked personnel records back at battalion headquarters. For example, he would have learned that this army mess sergeant had at one time been a famous chef at a popular New England resort. College-educated in home economics, Shirer had worked under such celebrated chefs as J. T. del Pietri of Paris, Aldo Belardini of Rome, and Hermann Wollin of Berlin, training that not only made him a superior cook but also a fair linguist.

But then things started going wrong for Brian Shirer. His wife died, the devil spawned Adolf Hitler, and his only two children were drafted into the army. Life was bitter. It hurt as only death can make it hurt. Shirer, however, had guts. Hit him and he hit back. "Little, yes, but tough," was the way one platoon sergeant described him. "Pop Shirer is as durable as a hunk of iron. The guy won't bend. His sons were killed, and in the back of his mind there's revenge. You wait and see. In his own way, in his own time, he'll even the score."

Meantime, Pop Shirer kept on turning out tasty food, which wasn't easy with a field kitchen—a truck loaded with canned goods, an oven on wheels, and a collection of pots and pans. If your chimney smoked, the enemy zeroed artillery shells in on you. If the men went hungry, morale turned bad. It was tough enough having to fight, without trying to do so on an empty stomach.

There were a couple of things that made Sergeant Shirer mad. Mostly, they had to do with supplies. Once a week provisions were delivered, sometimes by truck, sometimes by tank. Now that the 1st Infantry Division was doing its fighting in Europe, combat was more brutal. German troops were tough and knew the terrain. At times, roads became impassable because of gunfire. But the troops had to have food, so tanks were sometimes used to carry supplies, which was okay by Pop Shirer. It was *what* they occasionally dropped off at the field kitchen that upset Pop. Once they delivered two dozen floor mops, three cartons of rat poison, a gross of dishcloths, twenty-six scrub brushes, eighteen shoeshine kits, and sixty flyswatters.

"Look," Pop Shirer yelled at the men making the delivery, "I'm working in mud up to my butt and you give me floor mops. My boys are hungry and you deliver flyswatters."

Shouting did no good. He still got the rat poison, a squeezer for fresh oranges, and a dozen gourmet cookbooks. So he learned to take the good with the bad. The good he fed to the troops; the bad he somehow traded to natives for fresh vegetables, or whatever else they might have of nutritional value.

As the unit fought its way across the face of Europe, casualties became heavier. Pop Shirer suffered through having to feed a lot of new faces. Pop fed them, asked no questions, but searched each of their features hopefully. The men loved him for his wonderful meals. Secretly, behind his back, they conceded the mess sergeant was a little strange.

"Sort of off his rocker," Lieutenant Corns, a platoon commander said. "Got those watery blue eyes behind which you can't tell what's going on."

First Sergeant Pergrin added, "Trouble is, he's in a constant state of shock. Each replacement that comes along is one of his sons. So he feeds him with love and tenderness. Then he waits for the boy to return from combat. He's got something extra tasty prepared, but the boy doesn't show. Poof! he's gone and another replacement is standing in line."

Sergeant Brian Shirer wasn't without good friends. There was Corporal Opal and his squad of medical corpsmen. They hung around the kitchen area because it was warm. Opal was in charge of setting up a first-aid station. He and his men would stand nearby with their gear all marked by red crosses. When casualties began to arrive, they did their best to render emergency treatment. Then they shipped them on to the rear.

It was painful to watch a combat mission return. What was left of a platoon or company or whatever would head in one of two directions. Either they went to the medical aid station to get patched up, or they went to the kitchen to get food. Either way, they got good service.

It was after one such mission that Pop Shirer, Corporal Opal, and Olcheskie got to know each other. All of Europe was caught in the misery of a cold winter. It rained, it snowed it hailed. Most of Europe was a sea of mud. Hot food became more important than ever. Pop Shirer, on orders from the battalion commander moved his kitchen into what remained of a stone barn. It wasn't much—a basement that stank of cow manure and wet hay. Nevertheless, it did keep snow out of the cooking pots. That helped.

Then the battalion commander did something else. He raised so much ruckus at division headquarters, supplies came tumbling in. Big hams, crates of eggs, bread, cans of ground coffee, loads of vegetables, and concentrated soups. Sergeant Shirer was in hog heaven. Of course, along with the goodies came the irritants—mops, floor rags, rat poison, dustcloths, and china meat platters.

Sergeant Shirer complained to his friends Olcheskie and Opal. "They send me the makings for a cake and along with it these cans of rat poison. Are they trying to tell me something?"

"It's a new recipe, Pop," Opal said as he examined one of the cans of poison. "They send you nothing but the best. Look. This here label reads as follows: 'Extract of sodium fluoroacetate. Dangerous to all warm-blooded animals. White crystalline compound, odorless, tasteless. Soluble in warm liquids. Effective within thirty minutes.' "

Pop Shirer didn't laugh. He just looked off into space.

"You okay, Pop?" Olcheskie asked.

The mess sergeant snapped to. "Oh, ah, yeah. Sure. Just thinking up a new recipe."

"For what?"

"My favorite. Spice cake. Yeah, nice big pans of spice cake, washed down with hot coffee."

"You got the makings?" Corporal Opal asked.

"Sure enough. So tonight I'll bake maybe fifty trays of spice cake. Lots of cinnamon, butter, nutmeg, and sugar."

Pop Shirer never got to serve the Yankee troops his spice cake. The next day Germans slammed into a bulge in the line. They poured everything they had into it. Tanks, airborne troops, planes, and artillery. The Allies, caught by surprise, reeled back. Frontline troops tumbled into retreat. They resisted the Nazis with whatever they possessed. There was no time for food. The enemy overwhelmed them. Resist! Hold fast! It was impossible. The Germans had succeeded in mounting an irresistible attack.

Olcheskie was the last to see Pop Shirer. The old man was standing in the middle of his basement kitchen. He was surrounded by flat tins of fresh-baked spice cake and huge pots of coffee. He appeared to be stunned.

"Hey, Pop," Olcheskie yelled, "you better get out of here. Nazi panzer troops are just down the road, coming fast!"

Pop turned slowly. He stared at Olcheskie with those watery blue eyes. "No," he said. "I think I'll sit this one out."

"What the devil you mean by that?"

An 81-mm mortar shell thunked into a nearby field. After the splatter of mud, rock, and human rubbish had stopped falling, Sergeant Shirer said, "The troops will be hungry. German soldiers are human, too. They'll want something to eat."

Olcheskie was stunned. Just then Corporal Opal stuck his head through the door. "So long, you guys. We're moving the aid station."

"Hey Opal," Olcheskie called. "Pop's blown a gasket. He says he's going to feed the Germans."

"No good," the medic said. Then he was gone.

Machine gun fire raked what was left of the barn overhead. It was dangerously close. Olcheskie jerked at Pop's arm. "Let's go. Let's move."

The mess sergeant pulled his arm free. "No," he said. "I can't waste all this good food. The Germans will enjoy it."

Olcheskie could hear the rumble of tanks. They were Nazi tanks. A soldier could tell the cough of German diesel engines. "I'm moving, Pop. So long."

Time became a blur. Daylight and darkness intermingled with exhaustion and hunger. Olcheskie fell back with the rest of the troops. He found himself working a heavy machine gun. It ran out of ammunition. He retreated, helped carry ammunition for a bazooka team, and ended up working a walkie-talkie to assist in directing supplies air-dropped to the 101st (Screaming Eagle) Airborne Division. At this the combat reporter was good. His training as a newspaperman helped him see things in an objective light. The Germans outnumbered the Americans four to one. Nazi tanks and infantry overran Yank positions. Still the fighting continued. German artillery pounded isolated pockets of Allied forces. American P-47 fighter aircraft zoomed in. They caught long lines of Nazi supply trucks moving along narrow roads; they strafed. Then they located German tanks; these they bombed. The 9th and 10th Armored Divisions rallied to the aid of American infantry troops. The tide of battle turned.

*An enemy shell exploding this close
means it's time to change gun positions.*

If Olcheskie slept, he couldn't remember when. If he ate, it was out of a cold tin can. He ran into Corporal Opal.

"A shell struck our field hospital," Opal mumbled. "Only one doctor and myself survived."

"And now?" Olcheskie asked.

"Doctors, technicians, and medical supplies have been air-dropped. We're in good shape."

"So why not fall out and sleep for a while?"

Opal shrugged. "That fool Pop Shirer. I've got to see what's become of him."

They plodded along, silent, deflated, drained of energy, and half-starved. They came to a stretch of open terrain. Both recognized the area. Yes, there were the remnants of the stone barn. To get to it they had to step over hundreds of dead Germans. Corporal Opal was the first to notice that these corpses had a peculiar look about them. Opal dropped to his knees and thoroughly examined one of the cadavers. Then he went to another and did the same.

"Hmmm," he announced, "mighty strange. All these Germans appear to have died of a heart attack."

Olcheskie thought Opal had rocks in his head. He examined a body or two himself. No wounds. Just young men who had died. A peculiar story indeed. Now there was a medical officer. He, too, examined the bodies. "Yes," he confirmed, "it does seem as though they died of a thrombosis."

"Which is a heart attack?" Olcheskie asked.

"Yes, that is correct."

It was then they found Pop Shirer's body, seated at his cold field oven. In one hand he held a piece of sugar-dusted spice cake. In the other hand he clutched a mug of half-consumed coffee.

"Damn," Olcheskie growled as he stared around the basement kitchen, "Pop really fed the German troops. Look. All those tins of spice cake are empty. All that fresh-brewed coffee—gone."

Corporal Opal had other interests. He was examining the body of Sergeant Shirer. "Strange thing—Pop Shirer also died of a heart attack."

Olcheskie couldn't believe it. "Who ever heard of an epidemic of heart attacks? They aren't like a virus. They aren't contagious."

"Maybe not," Opal agreed, "but you're looking on what had to be an unarrested spread of heart attacks."

Olcheskie started pacing around the old cellar. He was feeling angry. Pop Shirer had let him down. He had fed the Nazis. He had given comfort to the enemy. What must his two dead sons be thinking of their father? Here was a story that must never be told. A Benedict Arnold with stripes on his arm.

"Damn, damn, damn, damn," Olcheskie cried out. There was a tin can underfoot. He gave it a vicious kick. There was another half-exposed can beneath the hay of the barn; he gave that a kick. This was one way of releasing pent-up emotions. He looked for more cans to kick. He saw them beneath the hay.

"Strange," he said out loud. Dropping to one knee, he uncovered a can, then another and another. He picked one up and studied the label; a smile broke out on his face. "God bless you, Pop Shirer. Darned if you aren't the greatest hero of them all."

"You say something?" Opal asked.

"Sure did," Olcheskie said, getting to his feet. He held out one of the cans. "You remember reading about that extract of sodium fluoroacetate?"

Opal nodded. "Rat poison. So what?"

"You didn't read far enough."

"How come?"

"Listen to this," Olcheskie said, reading from the label. " 'This poison acts on the heart. Death usually results from heart failure following ventricular fibrillation. Most successful when used with warm liquids.' "

"Wow!" Opal said, gazing about. "Good ol' Pop poisoned half a German division."

"Yeah," Olcheskie agreed. "By feeding them toxic spice cake washed down with deadly coffee."

"Quite a combination," Opal agreed. "A sure method for killing hungry troops."

"Out of my way," Olcheskie roared. He began to run toward the door. No longer tired, he was a man alive, a man with a mission.

"Where the devil you going in such a hurry?" Opal asked.

"To find a walkie-talkie. Man, I got a story that *has* to be told. Just wait till they catch my broadcast back at headquarters. It'll earn me another stripe."

"Yeah," Opal called. "And don't forget, Pop saved the last bite of cake and cup of coffee for himself. Just like a soldier saving the last bullet for his own brain."

Chapter Seven

"Unsung Hero"

Stick 'em with a bayonet and they bleed. A bullet in the head and they die. It doesn't matter when or where the war is being fought. A shell fragment kills as surely at Bull Run as it does at Pearl Harbor. Blood is as red at Anzio Beach as it is in the jungles of Kwajalein. War is war. The object is to kill. Men are called upon to banish other men from the earth. It's a grim, dirty business.

To the combat reporter war is also a spelling lesson. In World War II he learned that Holland's Arnhem was spelled with an *e* and not an *i,* and that Admiral Mitzumasa Yonai's name was spelled differently than it was pronounced.

So now it was Pohang-dong, Yandok, and Songin. Korea! A strip of land that lay between the Yellow Sea and the Sea of Japan. Americans died there, combat reporters included. Gathering news can be a dangerous pastime. The bayonet that kills a marine will as easily kill a reporter. A recoilless rifle cannot distinguish between the good guys and the bad guys, which is how Corporal Hoops Oliver came to be captured. A shell knocked him flat. He lost consciousness. When he came to, a little man with a big bayonet was standing over him. The tip of the bayonet pressed against Oliver's neck. It hurt. "Ouch," he said. The little man pressed harder. It hurt worse. It hurt almost to the point of death.

More little men clamored into the room. One brushed the bayonet aside, reached down, and jerked Hoops Oliver's wristwatch free. The two soldiers commenced to argue over the loot. A third man came in, obviously an officer. The men snapped to attention and froze. Words poured forth in an unintelligible stream. The officer took the watch and left. Oliver was yanked to his feet. The point of the bayonet flickered. It indicated something:Move! March! Get going!

It was raining outside. Icy water swept in off the mountaintop. The little men with big bayonets were not too well clad. One of them knocked Hoops down with a rifle butt and stripped him of his overcoat. Too stunned to protest, he was kicked by enemy soldiers till he struggled to his feet. They poked at him with their bayonets; he moved. There were other prisoners. He joined them and they began a death shuffle toward enemy country.

North Korea is a land of mountains. It is harsh country. There is no soft, yielding ground. All is sharp-pointed stone, thinly overlaid with soil. Roads are ledges hacked out of cliffs and covered with mud. Hoops' GI shoes, already worn from long usage, afforded little protection. He was a small, wiry man. There was no excess fat to be carried around; this was good. His ankles, however, turned on the sharp stones and he constantly stumbled. Each stumble earned him a jab from a bayonet.

More prisoners joined the column. Many had been stripped to the waist. They were practically freezing. Others were wounded. All were exhausted, battle weary, and stunned by the turn of events. The line grew in size and in suffering. A few prisoners couldn't stand the grind. When they fell, a guard rammed a bayonet through their neck and left them to bleed to death. One of the marchers was a medic. He wore a red cross on his left arm. A man close by was bayoneted. Instinctively, the medic dropped out of line to staunch the flow of blood. Another of the guards shot the medic through the head. Reverberating sounds of the gunshot brought an officer raging onto the scene. He waved his arms at the rifleman and slapped him in the face. Picking the empty cartridge off the ground, he shook it in the guard's face. It was clear the guard had earned himself a chewing-out for wasting ammunition. Then, as if to illustrate how killings should be done, the officer pulled a prisoner out of line. Snatching the rifle from the guard's hands, he drove the bayonet through the captive's neck. It was an unwarranted act of savagery. The prisoners broke ranks. They surged forward. There were rifle shots. Men dropped. Guards beat at their captives. When the prisoners fell back into line, the officer lay on the ground; there was an American trench knife sticking out of his chest.

This enraged the guards. Someone had been carrying a concealed weapon. The column was halted and everyone made to strip. Guards pillaged the mounds of clothing. Wallets, money, fountain pens, rings, watches, and other items of value were taken. What undergarments were left, prisoners put back on their shivering bodies. Night came early and with it sleet and hail. The prisoners huddled together for warmth and protection. It was a long, cold night.

In the morning, many of the men did not respond to bayonet prods. They were dead. To make sure, guards went among the prone and stabbed each with their bayonets. No playing possum here. Hoops Oliver consoled himself—he was not one of the dead. Yet neither was he altogether alive. His feet and ankles had swollen during the night, so that he had to unlace his shoes. His feet were on the verge of freezing. Guards went through the ranks handing out crusts of bread. Then the march was resumed. More fallen men, more bloodshed.

American fighter planes swept in low. They did not fire. It was obvious they recognized the column as being American prisoners. Pilots were not about to strafe their own kind.

There were more nights, more crusts of bread. Then the torturous march ended inside the walls of a prison. Two men to a tiny dungeonlike cell. Each cell faced onto a narrow corridor. There were cells lining either side of the passageway. At the open end of the hallway stood an armed guard. Silence was an absolute rule. To be heard talking meant to be dragged into the hall and beaten senseless. But then, for the first three or four days, no one *could* talk. The march had brought on complete exhaustion.

Hoops Oliver's feet bulged to enormous size. The skin cracked open and began to fester. He knew what it was—trench rot. Without medication and dryness, it could not be cured. Since neither of these things were to be had, his condition grew worse. He could no longer walk, only crawl. Nevertheless, his instincts as a reporter came to the forefront. He commenced to look about, to observe, even to hope.

His cellmate was a pilot whose plane had been shot down. The name he went by was Lank, for he was as thin as a reed and over six feet tall. Last names and military rank meant nothing here. Just staying alive was the thing. That could only be done by helping the other fellow, who in turn passed along his support.

For toilets, they were allowed one bucket per cell. With the coming of daylight, cells were opened one at a time. A single prisoner was then allowed to take the bucket aboveground for emptying into an open sewer. Once he accomplished this, the man had to return to his cell. Since Hoops Oliver could not walk, Lank was the one to go topside.

"What's it like up there?" Hoops asked in a whisper.

"Not much to see," Lank assured him. "We're only one of many underground barracks. I saw other prisoners emptying buckets further down the line."

"And is there a wall around this building?"

"No," Lank assured him, "just another building. Far beyond is the wall."

A guard came along. They shut up.

Through the bars of their cell door Hoops could see little. He could observe the cell straight across and the one to its left. There was only a wall to his right. His compartment and the one opposite marked the end of the corridor. This was good: no through traffic. The guards, being poorly supervised, seldom patroled to the extreme end of the passage.

There were other good and also some bad points to being imprisoned in this end cell. High up in the wall was a small air vent. This caused a constant draft of cold air. However, it did allow a certain amount of daylight to come into the cell. Gloom was not quite so constant. At times, sunshine found its way through the narrow opening. But the cold breeze was bad on Hoops' feet. He could no longer even stand. The pain was too great. He got about by walking on his knees.

It took time for Hoops and Lank to learn the facts about prison life. Even at that there weren't many facts to learn. The narrow passageway onto which their cell faced contained a total of sixty-four men. Some were in fair condition. Most were suffering from gunshot wounds, injuries, sickness, or trench foot. Occasionally the guards removed a man from the corridor. Sometimes, in heavily accented English, they would say, "To hospital." Other times they would take a man away without any explanation. Seldom did those removed ever reappear. At times men could be heard screaming. At other times firing squads could be heard. It was evident that both torture and murder were a part of this prison.

Whispering became an art. If words were murmured at just the right pitch, they could only be heard by cellmates in the immediate vicinity. Sign language was also popular. A whole alphabet of gestures, letters, and mimicry was developed. By such means, messages were transmitted throughout the cell block. Although real news was infrequent, rumors were constant. Prisoners were fed once a day. Meals generally consisted of soup made from fishheads and moldy rice. It was served by prisoners, who ladled it into each man's wooden bowl. "MacArthur—" they'd whisper, "he's marching north. Ought to be here any day now."

"Sissst, Charlie. You hear MacArthur's to reach here tomorrow?"

"No! Not tomorrow. Late today."

"You mean we ought to be free by tonight?"

"Yeah, sure. Why not?"

Disappointments were numerous. They were bitter and hard to swallow. However, for every rumor that expired, new ones developed. Occasionally one of the Communist guards would hear the whispering. Or perhaps he'd catch a man signaling with his hands. Other guards would be called and beatings administered. Sometimes a club would be used, at other times a bullwhip. In any event, it was sickening to see. Prisoners often died from these beatings.

"Morale is bad," Lank observed to Hoops. "We'll all die of a broken heart if something isn't done."

"Yeah," Hoops agreed. "But what?"

The beatings, the deaths, and the rumors continued.

"Sissst, Hoops!"

It was the guy in the cell immediately opposite, an infantryman named Kipper.

"Yeah?" Hoops acknowledged in a whisper, as he crawled to the bars of his door.

"Can you see anything through that vent?"

Lank heard him and went over to where the air vent was. He stood on his toes and raised his arm. The vent was just beyond fingertip reach. By sign he made it clear the opening was out of reach. Since there was no furniture in any cell, there was nothing to stand on.

Thinking came hard. Lack of food slowed mental processes. It was several days before Hoops came up with a solution. "Lank," he whispered, "I'll kneel under the opening; you stand on my shoulders."

The suggestion appealed to Lank. However, Hoops' bony frame didn't look as though it could support much weight. "You think you can hold my bulk?"

Hoops turned to the bars of his door. "Sissst, Kipper. Watch this. If you see a guard coming, give me a signal."

Crawling to a spot beneath the vent, he motioned Lank to climb. It was quite a struggle. Both men were frail and weak. After a tussle they managed to get Lank balanced on Hoops' shoulders. His eyes came to a level with the opening. They now had a peephole to the outside world.

"What'cha see?" Hoops gasped. His strength was running out. After a few moments he began to wobble. Then he folded and went flat.

Lank landed on his feet. For a moment he leaned against the wall. He appeared to be in shock.

"Sissst, Lank. See anything good?" It was Kipper calling. Hoops was just as impatient. "Yeah, Lank, what'cha see?"

Lank looked at them both. He smiled. It was a weak smile. "Yeah. I was just in time to see one of our Saberjets shoot down two Migs. They were away off in the distance."

"Migs? You mean them Russian-made fighter aircraft?"

"Yeah. Two of those fast Russian fighter planes the Chinese are using."

Instantly, the message was hissed around to every cell.

Word from the war front. Hot news. Yank fighter planes were knocking out the Communists. Morale went up.

The upsurge lasted two or three days. Then one of the prisoners in cell 4 had his right hand cut off as a punishment for stealing a crust of bread from a supply cart. The brutal act left the other prisoners in shock.

Each day, when the sun was about twelve o'clock high, Hoops would crawl to the vent. Lank would struggle onto his shoulders and for a few moments take a look. Frequently he could see no activity, or the weather was so bad it cut down on visibility. Then one day he saw a flight of American jets catch a column of enemy troops marching along a mountain road and zap, they were wiped out. The jets slaughtered the troops. The scene was so exciting Hoops insisted Lank take a second and third look. After that, what little strength he had was gone. He could no longer support Lank's weight.

Each day, the prisoners waited for Lank's report. It was like the issuing of a daily news bulletin. They lived from report to report. Some days there was no news at all. Other days, there were real headlines. Regardless, whatever the news, it was hissed up and down the passage. Men wanted to know what was going on outside. Here was their only hope. Even prisoners bringing in the soup wanted in on the news. They asked Lank for a description of the scene.

"There's a mountain off in the distance. A main road runs along its side. That's where the planes caught the troops. Out in the open and flat against the mountainside. What a beautiful slaughter."

"How many were killed?"

"Can't say. Impossible to give a body count. The mountain is too far away. I can just see the road and a railroad tunnel."

The food distributors gave Hoops an extra ladle of soup. They wanted his strength to increase. In fact, all the prisoners wanted to see him grow stronger. That was the weak link in this observation post. Hoops was not able to support Lank's weight for more than just a few moments. Then he would collapse. Some of the stronger men wanted to exchange cells.

"We can pull a switch on the guards during pot emptying time. Nobody will be the wiser. Then he can look out the vent for longer periods."

"No," Lank hissed. "The slightest suspicion and the guards will put a board over that opening."

His fears were logical. The guards had already noted an upsurge in spirits. They were also aware of an increase in whispering. To offset these things, they stepped up the number of beatings they handed out. But the secret of the peephole vent was preserved. Even the arrival of new prisoners failed to dampen the importance of Lank's observation post. These newcomers were replacements for those who had died or were taken away. They brought with them news. MacArthur had indeed launched an all-out invasion. South Korean troops, backed by American forces, were slicing a path through North Korea. Paratroopers were being used. Some might even be dropped on this prison compound as a rescue mission. Aerial gunships were now in use. These were prop-driven aircraft with banks of cannons. As strafing weapons they were tremendous.

Lank's observations confirmed these rumors. One day he caught a glimpse of a gunship strafing a supply train just as it was entering a tunnel. The entire string of freight cars burst into flames. This was grand news. Another day, far off in the distance, paratroopers could be seen floating down. Unfortunately, the prisoners were not rescued. Perhaps next time.

Sixty-four men lived on Lank's words. What he saw and relayed kept them alive. Hoops Oliver felt that his job of helping transmit the news was the most important journalistic assignment he'd ever had.

*Multiple rocket launchers fire
salvos of rockets at Communist targets
during an evening air attack.*

One day planes flew over the prison. There was the sound of aerial combat. The action was directly overhead. Prisoners pleaded with Lank to try and see what was going on. It had to be important; the guards had left their posts to join in the action. When they returned, anger was evident. They took it out on the prisoners. Several were almost beaten to death.

Two days later, the rescue began. American forces could be heard in the vicinity. Yes, Lank could see them on the mountainside. The guards were again withdrawn to join in the battle. Prisoners rioted. Hidden keys magically appeared and cell doors swung open. Men rushed to exit—just as the guards returned. There was gunfire.

Lank had been partway to the exit. He was one of the first hit. A bullet drove through his chest. Hoops Oliver crawled into the open and dragged Lank back to their cell. This kept a guard from sticking a bayonet through the wounded man. The painful effort on Hoops' part was useless; Lank died during the night.

The next day American soldiers arrived. All of a sudden they were there, guns blazing. The guards were wiped out. Then cell doors were ripped loose and men tumbled into the arms of freedom. But not Hoops Oliver. He was too crippled. Stretcher bearers were sent in after him, two jovial Yanks. What a welcome sight! "Come on, fellow," one of them said in words louder than a whisper, "we're here to carry you to the biggest roast beef dinner you've ever seen."

Hoops Oliver protested. "Just one thing," he said, "just one favor."

"Sure, man. You're on company time now. No hurry. What'cha want?"

"Lift me up and let me look through that air vent."

Both rescuers stared at him. "Crazy, man. Why waste time looking through a slit in the wall?"

"I'm a combat reporter. I've got the greatest story of my life. All I need is a look through that air vent."

Hoops was little more than skin and bones. One of the stretcher bearers hoisted him onto his shoulder and said, "So have yourself a good look."

Hoops took one look, said "My God," and fainted. The American soldiers lowered him to the stretcher. "Holy cow! I wonder what that poor guy saw? Whatever it was sure knocked the sand out of him."

It wasn't until three days later that Hoops Oliver revealed what he'd seen. An intelligence officer was questioning him about life as a prisoner of war.

"You say this Lank fellow was a hero?"

"Yeah, a real hero."

"What makes you say that?"

"He kept our spirits alive. He fed us hope when there was nothing to be hopeful about."

"Which was because he relayed what action he was seeing to the troops. Must have been a good view. You took a look. What did you see?"

"Nothing," Hoops answered, "absolutely nothing."

The debriefing officer reared back. "You must have seen something."

"Yeah. A blank wall. That air vent was almost flat up against the next building."

The startled officer gasped. "You mean—"

"Right. Lank kept us alive by pure imagination. He looked out that air vent and saw what we needed most. Hope. A little something to live for."

Chapter Eight

"Assignment Discovery"

Enemy infiltration! That was the new war gimmick the North Korean Communists were using. Hoards of people resembling refugees were sent fleeing south. In truth, they were trained spies and saboteurs: children carrying poison with which to contaminate public water supplies; old men capable of estimating the strength of American armed forces; beautiful women intent on seducing Yank soldiers; Communist troops uniformed as United Nations ground forces. They were all there, all on the loose.

Back in Tokyo, Japan, in the Meiji Building, a meeting was taking place. General Bill Knuckles had gathered forty of his best combat reporters together. They were divided into ten teams, called "flying squads." Each squad consisted of a writer, a still photographer, a motion picture cameraman, and a radio announcer. The object of these teams was to document the Korean War in its every facet—on land, sea, and in the air. It was a dangerous assignment. Go where the action was the hottest, record combat scenes on film, tape sounds of battle for broadcast, and write up what was actually taking place.

Lieutenant Bruno Woodstock headed one such team. He was a capable, aggressive, and tireless worker. On hitting Korea, he led his flying squad into action with the 31st Infantry Division. They recorded the miseries of trench warfare, the god-awful agonies of long marches through kneedeep mud, and the terrible boredom of hitching rides on freight trains that moved along at six miles an hour, if they moved at all. Squad members experienced the stink of their own unwashed bodies. They saw endless numbers of young Korean women placed against a wall and machine gunned. Spies! The Mata Haris of a new generation.

Dangerous war orphans were scooped up, found to be carrying poisons, and sent to the rear for corrective action. Recording these things wasn't pleasant work. There were fields scattered with dead. Entire villages were put to the torch.

Somehow, Lieutenant Woodstock found himself thrusting forward with the ROK (Republic of Korea) Capitol Division headed by General "Tiger" Song Yo Chan, an anti-Communist military leader of great capabilities. Tiger Song was pushing the Capitol Division into the heart of Communist country. He welcomed the presence of a flying squad.

"You have arrived just in time," he said, spreading a map before Lieutenant Woodstock. "Here is my main line of resistance." He drew a line across a series of mountains and valleys. "Beyond that, on this forward ridge, is my leading battalion. They in turn have placed one platoon on a hillock as our advance outpost. Beyond that, the platoon commander has entrenched a squad. All units are dug in and surrounded by barbed wire entanglements."

Woodstock understood. "General, on the face of it, I'd say your division is secure."

"Yes," Tiger Song agreed. But there was bitterness in his voice. "That isn't my concern."

"Oh? And what is it that troubles you?"

*This genteel-looking elder proved to be
a much-sought-after North Korean spy.*

"Not enough forward motion. I want victories, conquest. Sitting on our hands won't end a war."

Woodstock was taken aback by the emotion in Tiger Song's voice. "Well, ah, General, why not get going?"

The general smashed his fist down on the map. "Spies! Infiltrators! Informants! They're all around me. The Communists have even managed to place a spy on my staff. I can't plan a move but what the North Koreans don't get advance word of it."

"And how can my flying squad assist?" Woodstock asked.

"By documenting our every move."

"That's a big order. My stay here is limited to a day or so. Then I've got to shove along. There are other United Nations forces deserving coverage."

Tiger Song frowned. "Twenty-four hours. That's enough. The material you gather would allow me to analyze each step that has been taken. In that way, the spy might be uncovered."

"Like rerunning every play made in a football game?"

Song nodded. "Yes, exactly. Perhaps I will detect some hidden weakness."

Woodstock wasn't quite prepared for what he had stumbled into. That evening, General Song assembled his staff. There were three tough-looking Korean colonels present. They were introduced as Choi Kyu Hu, Nugeun Van Thieu, and Shim Bun Shik. In addition, present were three United Nations observers: Colonel Zeneke Asfaw, Ethiopian armed forces; Major Zenji Hatami, an American army officer of Japanese origin; and Major Mustafa Demir Cinel, of the Turkish air force.

Tiger Song had a wall map. He began his briefing. "As you know, my men are in these forward positions." He pointed them out on his map.

"They feel as though they are being used as live bait. To some degree this is correct. However, I have a plan. If we can lure the enemy into making an all-out attack against these forward positions, American artillery will lay down a heavy barrage. That should slaughter the Communists."

The officers present seemed to agree, so he continued. "Tonight, a reinforced platoon will move forward to relieve my men at the front. This force will shove off at 11:15 P.M. and be led by Captain Nguyen Du, one of my most capable officers."

The general hesitated. "This evening," he resumed slowly, "Captain Du will be fortunate in having along Lieutenant Bruno Woodstock and his team of combat reporters."

Lieutenant Woodstock was shocked. He'd made no such agreement! A night patrol into enemy territory? That was superdangerous stuff. Much too risky for a squad of newsmen. He was about to leap to his feet in protest, when those in the tent applauded. He looked around. There was respect and admiration in their glances.

"Nice going," Colonel Asfaw said.

"You Yanks are always into things," Major Cinel remarked.

Major Hatami, the American army officer, reached over and patted him on the back. "Nice going, fellah. I'm proud of you."

Woodstock felt boxed in by the brass. It was as if he'd been snared into this. Before he could protest, General Song called for Captain Nguyen Du. The man entered the tent. His presence grabbed everyone's attention. He was indeed a soldier ready to go on night patrol. His face had been blackened by burnt cork. His uniform was mud-colored and draped with a bandolier of hand grenades. There was a machine pistol, called a burp gun, hanging from one shoulder and a .45 automatic at his hip. Without wasting words, he picked up a pointer and turned to the chart. In heavily accented words, he said, "Here is our final objective, to relieve the men of this forward listening post."

Bruno Woodstock's eyes were as large as pie plates. The Korean captain was pointing to a spot far into enemy territory. This would be like entering a den of lions. No one seemed aware of his fears—least of all Captain Du. He continued talking. "Having relieved the forward position, we will then proceed to our secondary mission."

Secondary mission? Woodstock's heart almost stopped. My God, a single mission was enough for one night. Captain Du went on speaking. "We will then descend into the valley. There we will attempt to ambush an enemy patrol and take prisoners. After that we will withdraw."

There was a moment of silence. All present were studying the wall map. Bruno Woodstock could only see a maze of hills, valleys, and enemy gun emplacements. His mouth was dry, too dry to speak. He had a million questions he wanted to ask. Before he could pull his wits together, Captain Du said, "That concludes this briefing. It is now 9:15 P.M. This gives us time to prepare ourselves. If the American lieutenant will see me, I will help him ready his men."

Just like that. Bingo! The meeting broke up and everyone hurried out of the tent. Lieutenant Woodstock found himself being led into the night by Captain Du. Then there was the addition of burnt cork to the white of his skin, a belt laden with grenades, an automatic carbine, ammunition, and, of course, his personal .45 automatic handgun. While the men of his flying squad didn't welcome the assignment with joy, no one protested.

At exactly 11:15 P.M. the patrol moved into the night. To keep from getting separated, they held hands. Cling to the man ahead and let the man following cling to you. Hang on tight; to get disconnected could mean getting lost. And the night was tar-black—no stars, no moon, no ground lights, nothing.

And a spy back in camp. My God, Woodstock had forgotten all about that unknown factor. What if that person had already managed to alert the enemy that this patrol was en route? They would be butchered. He gripped the leading man tighter.

Suddenly a star shell climbed out of enemy territory. Woodstock knew what to do. Drop to the ground and freeze. Any movement would be visible. The star shell burst and the landscape was bathed in brilliant light. Not a sound. Nothing moved. All was quiet. Too quiet. The instant the light burned out, a machine gun rattled. It was somewhere in the distance. Rifles answered. There was the flash and bang of grenades. Captain Du was swearing. "They know we're here. They've been alerted."

"So we return?" Lieutenant Woodstock asked hopefully.

"No," the Korean captain said. "We must relieve our men in that forward position. They cannot be abandoned."

The column grabbed hands and resumed its forward push. They came to a stone wall. It was part of a drainage ditch leading to the valley. There were other trenches emptying into this main channel. Captain Du halted his column. He deployed his men along the low wall. On either flank he placed an automatic weapon. Then he called up a sergeant and signaled for a squad to move into the night. "They are the relief outpost. We now have only to wait. The old squad will rejoin us and we will withdraw."

This was the best news Woodstock had heard in years. "But what about prisoners? General Song wants prisoners for questioning."

Captain Du's voice was low. There was a mournful ring to his words. "The enemy knows we are here. They will jump

*A mortar crew fire their weapon and react
to the ear-splitting sounds that result.*

us soon. They will hit us in force. It is then we get our prisoners . . . or be taken prisoner."

Woodstock's heart was beating so hard he felt it could be heard by the enemy. He sneaked a look at the luminous hands of his wristwatch. Two-fifteen! My God, they'd been out there three hours!

Far across the landscape, an orange light split the skies. That meant the forward outpost had been relieved. They would be on their way back. Unfortunately, in the brief blink of that signal shell, a horrible sight was revealed. The silhouette of enemy soldiers could be seen closing in on the drainage ditch—riflemen with fixed bayonets. An automatic weapon burped. The enemy fired. Grenades burst. A bugle sounded. There was a deafening roar of rifle fire. Hand-held rockets ripped across the ground. A red star shell climbed into the sky and exploded. Heavy caliber artillery shells commenced to scream overhead. It was cannon fire leveled into the valley by American forces. The ground shook, dirt flew, action became a jumble of splitting light and intense blackness. The noise was deafening. There was cursing, yelling, and finally someone tugging at Woodstock's sleeve. It was Captain Du. "Now we withdraw."

"Prisoners?" The lieutenant gasped.

"Too late. Enemy has us almost surrounded. They'll be attacking in force. Let's get out of here."

Easier said than done. The Communists had them pinpointed. Machine guns raked their position. Mortar shells rained down on them. It was dangerous going. By the time they reached their own lines, it was turning daylight. Woodstock went amidst the survivors trying to find his own men. Two were missing. A pair of good reporters, gone. He was angry and full of hate for the world.

Both Captain Du and Lieutenant Woodstock were summoned to the headquarters tent. A debriefing would take place immediately. Colonel Hu and a number of other Korean officers, the Ethiopian colonel, the Turkish officer, and Major Hatami were on hand. Colonel Hu seemed to be in charge. "General Song will join us for this debriefing. However, he has been delayed for a few minutes."

Woodstock was so angry and uptight, he shouted at those present, "We were betrayed. The enemy knew we were coming. They knew exactly where to look for us. It isn't hard to figure; there's a spy in your midst."

Major Hatami pulled Woodstock onto one of the camp chairs. "Easy does it. This is a debriefing, not a complaint session."

Woodstock threw aside the extra weapons he was carrying. It was stuffy inside this crowded tent; he opened his overcoat. Instinctively he patted the .45 in his shoulder holster. How he would like to know who that spy was now!

Colonel Hu spoke again. "The general will be here at any moment. Meantime, relax. Smoke if you wish. Have coffee."

Major Hatami moved to sit beside Woodstock. "Look," the major said, "we all know how you feel. But play this spy stuff low key. It's a sore point with General Song."

Woodstock stared at the American major. He didn't like what was being said. "You're Nisei?"

"Right," Major Hatami said. "Both my parents were Japanese."

Nisei, as they both understood, meant any Japanese born in the United States. "Where in the States were you born, Major?"

"Philadelphia," Hatami replied.

Woodstock smiled. It was the first time he'd smiled in a long time. "Son-of-a-gun, so was I. In fact I graduated from the University of Pennsylvania, in downtown Philly."

Hatami seemed glad to note that Lieutenant Woodstock was calming down. "Yeah? Good ol' Philly. Wish we were both there right now. And oh, by the way, as I said a moment ago, I wouldn't push that idea of a spy. General Song is a very unpleasant guy whenever it's referred to."

Woodstock appeared to have forgotten combat. There was a dreamy look in his eyes. Philadelphia had apparently taken over his thoughts. "Where'd you go to school, Major?"

"Temple University," Hatami answered.

"Oh yeah, sure. A great school. Out on West Broad Street."

Hatami was obviously satisfied to have distracted the lieutenant's anger. "Yeah. I lived out on West Broad Street. Stayed in a rooming house out that way."

Woodstock chuckled. "Boy, oh boy, how I wish we were in Magillan's Old Ale House on East 15th Street. Remember that? Quite a student hangout."

Major Hatami laughed. "Yeah. We used to have some great times there."

Before anything further could be said, General Song entered the tent. Everyone got to their feet.

"Be seated, gentlemen," the general growled. It was obvious he was in an ugly mood. The night patrol had not gone well. No prisoners had been brought back for questioning. Casualties had been heavy. Now he wanted answers.

Everyone took their seats except Woodstock. He remained standing. All eyes swung to look at him. Now what? Colonel Hu cleared his throat. "Ah, ahem, Lieutenant Woodstock, you may be seated."

It was as if Woodstock had not heard. Slowly, deliberately, he took out his .45 automatic. Gripping it by the handle, he turned to Major Hatami and held the gun to the man's head.

"What is that for?" Tiger Song roared as he moved toward Woodstock. "Have you gone mad?"

"No," Woodstock answered. "You wanted a prisoner to question. Well here's one. He's a spy."

"A spy? What makes you say that?"

Woodstock was obviously feeling better now. "There's no West Broad Street in Philadelphia. Broad Street's the main drag and it runs north and south. Furthermore, there isn't a Temple University student who doesn't know where Magillan's Old Ale House is. It can't be found on East 15th Street. That street runs north and south too."

Woodstock holstered his .45. "If you examine his credentials, I'm sure you'll find they're counterfeit."

They did. And they were.

Chapter Nine

"The Convert"

Battle orders were clear. The 1st Battalion of the 12th Infantry was to proceed to the Me Wei area. Alpha ("A") Company and Delta ("D") Company were to assist in the fighting taking place in that sector.

First Sergeant Sledge Baldwin of Alpha didn't like Choo-choo Quincy of Delta. Sledge was big, brutal, and not very brainy. Choo-choo was short, slender, and smart. The big guy confined his reading to the company roster, orders for the day, and racing sheets showing the daily double being run at Saigon. His cultural activities were limited to beer drinking and shooting the breeze with the boys. The small man was into such things as philosophy, poetry, and psychic powers—topics that came out of books, heavy stuff that had nothing to do with gunfire. He liked Brahms, Plato, and cold lobster en coquilles.

There were other difficulties, too. Sledge Baldwin was a professional soldier. The army was his life, and he enjoyed combat. Vietnam, to him, was a playground, and he was happy to be there. Choo-choo Quincy was a draftee. He hated military life, detested combat, and abhorred Vietnam. The only thing that tied them together was Baldwin's marriage to Quincy's sister.

As luck would have it, Alpha Company and Delta Company were always being thrown together. Their unit commanders got along just fine. As a reinforced combat team, they were effective under fire. As for instance on that day the Vietcong pinned Alpha down with small arms, automatic weapons, and mortar fire. Somehow, in some mysterious manner, the commander of Delta sensed the difficulty and came to the rescue.

"Extrasensory perception," Choo-choo claimed. "The two have ESP. Their minds are in harmony with one another."

"Bull," Sledge growled. "It's probably radio communications what done it. This here psychic stuff won't stop no bullets."

The two in-laws had come across one another in a filthy, leech-infested rice paddy. They now stood kneedeep in muck while they argued their beliefs. A sniper's bullet buzzed between them. That ended the discussion. Both scurried toward safer ground.

The fighting around Me Wei was different from anything previously experienced. It was more than just plain brutal; it was inhuman. The Vietcong were hiding in jungles that could neither be penetrated nor avoided. The terrain consisted of mountain ranges matted with dense vegetation and valleys puddled with large swamps. The air was so stifling that days under 110 degrees were considered comfortable.

And all this greenery was the breeding ground for millions of living horrors that crept, oozed, clung, or itched. Yet the Vietcong lived there. They had villages so heavily shrouded by vegetation they could neither be seen from the air nor located on a map. There was only one way to find them. Screen them out by "recon-in-force," which meant that a large number of troops would be spread in a line to comb the jungle. With luck they might locate and destroy some of the enemy.

Generally, however, the Vietcong would hear them coming and abandon their villages to old women, children, and graybeards too rickety to hold a weapon. So the Americans would return to their base camp with very little accomplished, exhausted, and with their ranks frequently depleted by dead or wounded.

The next day another reinforced combat team would be sent out. Perhaps it would be made up of Bravo ("B") Company and Charlie ("C") Company. To speed things up, men might be airlifted by helicopter, or transported to a distant starting point by truck. But it was always to plunge into the impenetrable jungle. They were forever searching after the lair of the hidden Vietcong.

Tactics varied little. The hammer-and-anvil technique was generally used. A column entered the jungle and beat the brush as they hacked through the timberland. This would flush the enemy into the waiting arms of the second column —the nutcracker effect. Sometimes it worked. More often it did not. The VC possessed hidden tunnels and secret trails. They just seemed to fade away.

All too often the Vietcong played their own tricks. They would lead a combat unit deeper and deeper into the jungle. When the Americans were hidden from view and in such thick jungle that radio communications were lost, bang!—that's when the VC would strike in force. The Yanks, being out of touch, were then on their own. An intense firefight would follow.

After hours of bloody fighting, the Americans were generally able to force their way into an open area. Radio com-

*A recon-in-force movement against
Vietcong hiding in the jungle.*

munications could be reestablished and close air support flown in. With luck, reinforcements would also arrive.

Corporal Quincy had a theory about the enemy. "Lookit," he would preach to anyone listening, "they're using ESP, that mental telepathy stuff."

"Tell me more," the regimental intelligence officer once said to him with a sneer. "How's it work?"

"We know the Russians have been doing laboratory experiments with extrasensory perception. If people are in mental harmony, they can send thought messages to one another. So they've trained the Cong to send warning messages through the jungle."

"You mean," the officer prodded, "the enemy is onto something better than radio?"

"When it works, yes," Choo-choo Quincy said. "Nothing can stop ESP. One man has a thought; it can be transmitted halfway around the world to another person. That is, of course, if the two are in harmony."

"And how do the Vietcong know when they got two people in tune with each other?"

Corporal Quincy was patient. The regimental intelligence officer was a real skeptic. Perhaps that's why he was a good intelligence officer. He doubted the truth about everything. "Sir," Choo-choo said, "ESP works best between related people in time of stress, like perhaps brother and sister, husband and wife, distant cousins. . . ."

"We haven't any American women out here in the bush, Corporal, so ESP wouldn't work for us."

Choo-choo Quincy was annoyed. The officer was simply harassing him. "Not necessarily between male and female. Thoughts can be broadcast from one man to another."

For a moment it seemed as though the intelligence officer was beginning to take an interest. "Hmmmmmm," he intoned, "aren't you getting into stuff like astrology, premonitions, and survival of the soul?"

"Absolutely," Quincy agreed. "The overall package is called psychic knowledge."

This was too much for the intelligence officer. "See the chaplain," he said with a wave of his hand. "Don't be bothering me with your ESP theories; I got a war to fight."

So Choo-choo had to live alone with his unconventional beliefs. "You got rocks inside your skull, Choo-choo. Whyn't you put more thought into shooting the enemy?" said Sergeant Baldwin.

Which is the way things went. About once a week Alpha and Delta Companies would be formed into a task force. Then out into the jungle they would go, to fight a war that would never be won.

One day a warning order was received. At 0600 hours (6 A.M.), a combat team made up of A and D Companies was to be ready for airlift. It was to go on a special "search and destroy" mission. The intelligence officer passed the word. "Air reconaissance has spotted the headquarters of a large Vietcong force hidden in the jungle. American units will be airlifted to the nearest open space by helicopters and off-loaded. After that it will be a hammer and anvil operation."

At first, things went as planned. However, as always in combat, action became jumbled under fire. Units got scrambled, orders got mixed up, and many unforeseen events occurred. Early in the action, the commanding officers of both Alpha and Delta got hit. They had to be airlifted out. The action continued, more men got chopped down, ranks were thinned by rifle fire. Still, they endured. The Yanks were tough fighters, persistent and well armed. They pushed on.

First Sergeant Baldwin found himself leading a unit. It

*Soldiers advance in correct military style
down a road through enemy territory.*

was what remained of one platoon from Alpha and one platoon from Delta. No officers were left standing. All had been wounded and taken out by helicopter. But Baldwin was as good as any captain, and better than most. Self-confident, experienced, he knew his enemy and was wise to many of their tricks. Unfortunately, he came up against one of the oldest military problems known to exist in the history of warfare—one never successfully resolved even by such greats as Julius Caesar, Napoleon Bonaparte, or George Washington. They were at the foot of a mountain; the troops had to go around. If the column was led to the right, enemy forces might be coming from the left. That meant they would strike oncoming troops in the flank. This would be hitting at the weakest point. If the troops were led to the left, the reverse could be true. On the other hand, if advancing troops were to be split in half and sent around both sides of the mountain, the enemy would then have only part of the force to battle.

Sledge Baldwin wasn't sure what to do. The land mass was too high, too overgrown with jungle, and too likely to be capped by enemy bunkers to climb over. Off to the right was a river. Perhaps fifty yards wide, it was swift-running, slimy, and loaded with poisonous snakes. However, it did offer some protection against enemy attack and there were some precautions he could take. So that's the way he chose.

"Send up that crazy in-law of mine, Choo-choo Quincy," he told a platoon sergeant.

When Choo-choo arrived, Baldwin said to him, "You're a radio man. I want you to take a walkie-talkie off to the left of this mountain. Reinforce yourself with a squad of riflemen. Go about a quarter-mile along the foot of the mountain. There stand lookout. If you see the enemy coming, let me know."

Choo-choo nodded. "Sure. But with you on one side of the mountain and me on the other, radio contact will be lost."

"Okay," Baldwin said. "Keep in touch as long as you can. I'll have Flip McGee on another walkie-talkie. He'll be with me."

Which is the way they left things, Sledge Baldwin shoving off to the right, Choo-choo to the left. It was tough going for both. Hacking a path through the dense underbrush was beastly work. They could only make about one mile per hour. All the while, they kept in touch.

"Bird One," Choo-choo would call over the air. "Do you read me?"

"Roger that, Bird Two. You're weak but readable," Flip McGee would reply.

Sergeant Baldwin finally reached the river. He pushed ahead. Now he was leading the troops between the stream and the face of the mountain, parallel to the swift river. It gave him a bad feeling. If the enemy should strike from across the stream, he'd be in trouble. They'd be able to crush him against the side of the mountain. Unfortunately, it was too late now to back down; he had committed his forces.

"McGee," the sergeant called. "What do you hear from Choo-choo?"

"Nothing," Flip McGee said. "We lost him ten minutes ago."

Darn, Sledge Baldwin thought to himself. This made things worse. Now his rear was open to attack. Not likely that would happen, but he had to be aware of the possibility. He waved his column of troops onward. The heat inside those jungles was enough to cook a man's brains. That and the bugs. They attacked each soldier in swarms. Slowly, penetratingly, the Yanks slogged across swamplike ground. At times they were hip-deep in ooze and muck that sucked at their boots with every step.

Sergeant Baldwin raised his hand. "Take a break," he

called back along the column. "But stay alert. We're in the enemy's zone of action."

While the troops dropped out of formation, Baldwin gave some thought to his situation. He had maybe two hundred men behind him. They were a leftover sort of organization. Not much fire power. They only carried a few mortars, machine guns, and bazookas. Also, if he weren't careful, the troops would shoot off all their ammo before actually closing with the enemy, which meant he couldn't rake the opposite riverbank with small-arms fire. And that he didn't like. If the enemy were hiding over there, an outpouring of bullets would bring answering fire. On the other hand, maybe the Vietcong were not even aware the Yanks were so close.

"McGee," he called. "How long have we been out of touch with Bird Two?"

Flip McGee studied his wristwatch. "Lemme see. It's now eleven-fifteen. We ain't had no word from Choo-choo since ten-fifty-five. That there's twenty minutes."

"And we can't contact headquarters?"

"No way, Sarge. That's a good ten miles off. This radio won't never cut through that much jungle."

"Any chance of Choo-choo getting word to us over the top of that mountain?"

"Nup," McGee said. "Sarge, we're isolated and that is that."

Sergeant Baldwin felt an awful loneliness. Nowhere to turn for advice. No one to call upon for help. Decisions were his to make or not to make. Now it was either push ahead or turn tail and run. "Okay you guys. On your feet. Let's push ahead."

The forward movement commenced again. Elephant grass and bamboo grew so thick the head man had to chop his way with a machete. Those who followed threw themselves against the walls of thicket to broaden the path. Silt, slime, and ooze continued to be part of the scene. Bugs, snakes, and vicious underbrush varmints had to be dealt with. The column pushed forward slowly, ever aware that the river was squeezing them closer to the side of the mountain. They were in a deadly situation.

Suddenly Choo-choo's voice popped out of the radio. "Baldwin, this is Quincy. Halt! Stop! You're walking into a trap!"

The clarity and loudness of Choo-choo's words jerked Flip McGee and Sledge Baldwin to a halt. "Holy cow, you hear that, Sarge?"

Baldwin was both amazed and annoyed. "Thought you said his radio couldn't reach us."

"Well, ah, it can't. What I mean is, it shouldn't be able to."

Baldwin was nettled by the tone of Choo-choo's voice. A corporal giving a combat-hardened sergeant orders. And him on the other side of the mountain! "How's he know what we're up against?"

Flip McGee was only a private. He didn't want to get into any discussion about tactics. "Gosh, Sarge, I don't know. It seems to me—"

"Flatten your men, Sledge. Quick! I called for a barrage of heavy artillery to hit that riverbank." It was Choo-choo's voice again, clear, crisp, and very assertive.

Sledge Baldwin was steaming mad. "That knothead. He's playing games with us. I'll have him court-martialed for this. There ain't no way he can tell what's going on over here."

"Yeah," Flip McGee agreed. He was picking up a bit of Baldwin's anger. "And besides, he ain't got a radio with enough power to reach headquarters. So how's he going to—"

Scareeeeeem! A shell from an 8-inch howitzer passed close overhead. With a thunderous roar, it exploded on the far shore. Then a shell from a 155 howled in. Soon, every imaginable type of American artillery was zeroed in on the enemy side of the river. Long-range 18-inch rifles and big-time howitzers had an input. Gigantic shells from 240 mm howitzers, firing in tandem, shook the earth. Beehive shells tore enemy jungle into shreds. These beehive shells were made to burst over a target and spray darts.

Baldwin stood in amazement as bodies and weapons came flying out of the distant brush. Vietcong were caught in a boiling cauldron of artillery fire. To flee, many leaped into the river. Anything to get away from the thunderous onslaught.

"Fire!" Baldwin yelled. The noise was too great for his voice. He used hand signals. His men had a clear field of fire. The enemy could plainly be seen leaping into the river. Yanks opened up with everything they had. Automatic rifles, .50 caliber machine guns, bazookas, and hand grenades.

It was a turkey shoot.

By the time artillery fire ceased and Sergeant Baldwin got his men off their triggers, they'd wiped out a major Vietcong attack force. Friendly planes flew overhead. They circled the area and took off to strafe the fleeing enemy. Radio communications were again established. A C & C chopper (command and control helicopter) flew in three colonels and a general. When they landed and discovered Sergeant Baldwin in charge, they lavished praise on him.

This was fine with Sledge Baldwin. But it was really Choo-choo who'd pulled off this entrapment. The mystery was, how'd that little guy know what the enemy was up to? Besides, even if he did know, how was he able to call down artillery fire on a pinpoint target? By gosh, he was going to find Choo-choo and get a few answers.

Several days went by before Sergeant Baldwin got his troops back to home base. Then he went looking for Choo-

choo Quincy. Delta company was being re-formed. A lot of replacements had arrived. Not many knew of a Corporal Quincy. The name didn't strike a bell. One man offered some help. "Yeah," he told Baldwin, "I remember the guy. He was a squinty little runt always quoting Shakespeare an' Longfellow an' Walt Whitman an'—"

"Yeah, yeah," Baldwin interrupted, "so what's become of him?"

The fellow shrugged. "Don't know. Heard he got WIA (wounded in action). Maybe you could find out something from the medics."

Sergeant Baldwin suddenly developed an icy feeling around his heart. He hurried to the hospital tent. No word. Nothing. A corpsman had a suggestion. "You should check out the chaplain."

Seeing the chaplain only made it worse. "Yeah. They brought him in on a helicopter. He was KIA (killed in action). We already shipped his body to a rear mortician."

Baldwin felt like he'd been bashed on the head with a mallet. "How'd he get hit?"

The chaplain shrugged. "Sorry, I don't know about such things. My records only indicate that a chopper from medical evacuation brought him in. Maybe you should talk to the chopper crew chief. A nice guy named Armstrong, Sergeant Joe Armstrong."

The crew chief was nice enough. "Sure, I remember that Corporal Quincy. Or at least I remember seeing what was left of him. An enemy mortar shell struck the walkie-talkie he was hunched over."

Sergeant Baldwin was beginning to feel quite strange. "You keep a flight log?"

Joe Armstrong said that he did. He kept a detailed log. "Like to see it?"

One look and Sergeant Baldwin said, "Thanks. I got to get back to that chaplain I was talking to."

The chaplain was a youngish man, busy but not so busy he couldn't afford to spend a few moments with a soldier obviously emotionally upset. "Did you find that air evac crew chief named Armstrong?"

"Yeah. Now I'm turned inside out."

"How's that, Sarge?"

"Armstrong's log shows they picked up Corporal Quincy's body at ten-thirty that morning."

"So?" the chaplain asked.

"Then how could Quincy's voice come over the radio some time after eleven that same day?"

The chaplain looked hard and steady at Baldwin. "Sergeant, do you believe in clairvoyance?"

Sledge Baldwin shook his head. "I don't even know what the word means."

"Well," the chaplain said slowly, "you were party to a form of what is known as extrasensory perception."

"ESP?" Baldwin gasped.

"Why yes. Do you believe in that?"

Sergeant Baldwin turned and started to walk away. Then he swung around. There were tears running down his cheeks. The hardness had gone out of him. He was just another GI suffering from battle fatigue.

"There was a time when I didn't. But I do now."

Chapter Ten

"Farmer in the Dell"

They lay in the drainage ditch and planned their next move—
Butwell, the combat reporter; and Scripta, the squad leader.
Behind them sprawled eight battle-weary GIs. All they wanted
was to make it back to their unit. No more fire fights. They'd
put in a night of horror. Mortar bombs, rockets, artillery fire,
star shells, tracers, and grenades. It was like trying to stay
alive in a shooting gallery gone berserk.

Now the sun was coming up. It peered over the horizon
in a hesitant manner. It was as if the gods hated to light this
awful carnage called Vietnam. So as a mark of protest they
painted the sun red. This turned the flooded rice paddies into
vast pools of what looked like blood. Off to the left lay B
Company's perimeter; that meant safety. Off to the right
could be seen a village; that meant death. The squad was
equidistant from each.

"The next hour," Sergeant Scripta said softly over one
shoulder, "will set the pattern for the day."

Corporal Butwell noted that the sergeant had been keep-
ing a close watch on the village. "Sarge," he said, "the next

hour could mean more than that. It could mean life or death for Moir and Vose."

The sergeant took his gaze off the village and looked at the reporter. It was a cold, frosty look. Although the sergeant wore a helmet, flak jacket, and combat boots, all visible parts were layered over with mud. It was hard to recognize him for what he was—a nineteen-year-old squad leader who had dropped out of high school to enlist in the army. Tough, yes. That and battle-wise.

"Butwell," he said. "Moir and Vose got hit. Too bad. So we give 'em first aid and watch over 'em. A little extra attention. But you ain't getting that special attention. Now my suggestion is you worry about your own hide. Not theirs."

Good point, Butwell conceded. As a reporter, he knew nothing concerning battle survival. Last night showed him that. He'd gone out with this detail, which had been ordered to man a forward listening post. His object had been to learn what such a mission was like during hours of darkness. He'd found out. Noise! Earth that quivered from bomb blasts. Men screaming in agony. The overhead shriek of small-arms fire. Who needed a listening post for this? The sounds could be heard for miles.

"Lookit," Scripta had explained between onslaughts, "our object is to watch for enemy soldiers. They creep into these villages at night. The women feed them. Come the first crack of dawn, like right now, they slip back into the bush. We try to nail them en route."

"What about the women?" Butwell asked. "What happens to them?"

"We ain't allowed to shoot no women. They only work the rice paddies. So they gets safe passage."

Butwell lay in the stinking mud and thought about these things. The village off to his right appeared to be quiet at the moment. He could see a spirelike pagoda surrounded by thatched huts. A poor example of a village. A few months ago it had been encircled by trees and bushes. Now there were only ragged stumps and charred embers. That and a handful of shacks made of flattened tin cans, thatch, and cardboard. Hard to believe, a hundred or more people still lived in these shambles.

"Hey Eagle-eye," Scripta called. "Come up here, man."

One of the prone figures began to crawl forward. He was copper-colored and looked like the Indian on a nickel. There was an old-fashioned bolt-action Springfield rifle in his grip. "Yeah, Sarge?"

"Take a look. Let me know what you see."

Eagle-eye crawled to the crest of the ditch. While he looked, the sergeant dropped back a bit. Taking out a canteen, he sipped at the brackish water. "That guy," he said jerking a thumb in Eagle-eye's direction, "is Cherokee Indian. He's got eyesight like they ain't never been able to build into binoculars."

"Why the bolt-action rifle? Why not an M-16?" Butwell asked.

"Says he can work off one shot better with a bolt-action. And that's all he needs. A single crack at the enemy and he's dead. If he fires off any more, they might spot his muzzle blast and unload some mortars on us."

Eagle-eye twisted his head. "Hey, Sarge, a single . . . in pajamas . . . doing the infantry crouch."

The infantry crouch was a bent-over stance, a figure running as if not wanting to be seen. "Knock him," Scripta said.

The Indian took off his helmet and let it slide down to the sergeant. Then he thumbed loose the safety and nestled his cheek alongside the rifle stock. There was a wait that seemed needlessly long. Suddenly a rifle blast.

"Get him?" Scripta asked.

Eagle-eye slithered down. "Naturally," he said with a grin. "But there's maybe three or four pajamas off'n to the left. Could be they're working at setting up something heavy."

"Hmmmmmm," Scripta said. It was obvious he was doing some thinking.

Butwell was confused. "Why pajamas? How's that set them apart?"

Eagle-eye gave a halfway smile. "Enemy. They wear black cloth that fits them like pajamas. The women dress different. They wrap themselves in colored cloth, wear big pointed straw hats, and show pigtails."

Butwell thought about this. It made sense. The women had to work in the fields all day, under the hot sun. They needed the protection of big hats.

"Radio," Scripta called as he crawled to the lip of the ditch.

A soldier crept forward holding a walkie-talkie. He lay alongside Sergeant Scripta. "Yeah, Sarge?"

"Contact headquarters. I want to talk to 'em," Scripta said.

The man with the radio put in the call and was answered. He handed the mouthpiece to Scripta, who pressed the button and said, "This is A-4. I got me some action. Lone tree, azimuth three-three-zero. Lower me about six shots of heavy. And keep in mind, no short rounds. We're between you and that target."

Again there was a wait. The sergeant beckoned Butwell alongside. He was smiling. "The enemy don't know we're here. They think they can't be seen from our perimeter."

Butwell was amazed. "But Sarge, why'd they blast this field last night?"

Scripta chuckled. "You ain't never going to make a combat infantryman. First thing, you got to learn to think like the enemy."

"Which is?" Butwell prompted.

"There's no way they know we're out here. So when they shoot off a lot of ammo like that, it's to clear a passage of any possible land mines."

Butwell was beginning to get the message. "You mean," he gasped, "we're astride their line of escape?"

Before Scripta could answer, there was a thunderous explosion, then another and another. "Right on the money," the sergeant yelled into the radio. "You creamed 'em."

He gave a hand signal to the men sprawled at the rear. They commenced to crawl along with him. They moved toward the village, away from their own company compound.

"Hey Sarge," Butwell called. "Aren't you going in the wrong direction?"

Scripta turned long enough to say, "If you want to survive, man, you got to outthink the enemy. If'n you head toward home base, they'll bite you in the rear. Our only chance is to locate their main column. That way we can order a load of mortar shells to be dumped on 'em."

Ttere was daylight now. The sun was up. With it came heat and stink. The odors from the rice paddies began to rise. These fields were fertilized by human waste. It stunk with gagging ferocity.

The detail inched along. They kept low and quiet. After a bit, the drainage ditch came to a fork. The sergeant halted and appeared to be thinking. No doubt he was trying to reason like the enemy. Which ditch would they use? How many would be there?

Immediately to Scripta's rear came Eagle-eye. He had a trench knife between his teeth. It made him look like a pirate. Behind him crawled the man they called Radio. He appeared to be about twenty, and scared. After that was Butwell, plus the rest of the squad. Five to ten feet lay between each man. If a shell hit, they wouldn't all be wiped out.

That had been Moir and Vose's problem. Last night they'd been hunkered close. One shrapnel burst got both.

Now everyone lay still. They were frying under a hot sun. It was like being in a steambath wearing heavy underwear. Still Scripta waited. He seemed to be listening, sniffing the air. Something was wrong. Butwell could feel it in his gut. Oh God, would this patrol never end? It was supposed to have been a night patrol. Now it had extended into a day patrol. They should have been relieved hours ago. It was this guy Scripta—he was too eager, always wanting to be a good soldier, forever attempting to prove himself.

Abruptly an enemy soldier reared up from the bottom of a gully. He lunged at Scripta with a bayoneted rifle. Not quick enough. With the sweep of one hand, Eagle-eye sent his trench knife flying through the air. THUNK! It struck the man in the chest. He tottered for a moment, a surprised look on his face. Then he fell over backwards, dead.

Scripta moved fast. He crawled to the dead man. Grabbing the man's rifle, he examined the chamber. It was loaded. For a moment or so he gave this fact some thought. Why had the man not shot him? Interesting question. He pulled the trench knife free and tossed it to Eagle-eye. Then he returned to his squad.

"Radio," he called in not too loud a voice. "Get the OP (operations post) and tell 'em we've made contact. Make sure they get a fix on us with their radio finder."

Using hand signals, he placed his riflemen. All were facing the village. Then he signaled Butwell to come close. "Get yourself a rifle. We're in for some action."

Butwell was both tired and frightened. He had never been in a fire fight. His view of a battlefield had always been from a distance. Now this kid, this so-called sergeant, had landed him in the soup. This made him angry. "Why can't we just pull out and leg it back to the perimeter?"

Scripta was startled at the annoyance in Butwell's voice. He looked at the reporter and thought about what had been said. That was Scripta's way. Think about everything. Act on logic. What would the enemy do next? Why had this man snapped back at him? There were always answers to these questions. He let a half-smile creep across his mud-splattered face. "Reporter fellah, you leg it for the perimeter and you're doing just what the enemy wants you to do. The object of this here game is to do what they don't expect. That way you'll survive."

Theory. Guesswork. "Sergeant, I don't see any enemy. There's nothing out there but rice paddies."

Scripta was staring at the distant village. He talked without turning his head. "Why do you think that guy didn't gun me down? Cause a bayonet kills without making noise. Which means he didn't want our main force to know he's out here. Now that tells me a lot. Somewhere, between you, me, and that village is a bunch of creeps trying to make it back to the bush."

Butwell hadn't thought about that. Nevertheless, he didn't approve of these tactics. "A standoff," he said. "So we let them go and they let us go."

"Fair enough," Scripta said. "You got my permission to go out there and negotiate with them."

Butwell licked his lips. This kid was truly a hard nut. But maybe there was some logic to the way he thought. The sergeant was still watching the village. "Reporter," he said without turning, "you want to make a run for the perimeter across those flats, fine. You go ahead. Just what we need, a decoy. They'll shoot at you and reveal their position, which is what we need."

After a moment he added, "And if you make the perimeter, Reporter, tell the captain you ran off and left the wounded. The boys back there would appreciate knowing that."

Butwell licked his lips. He couldn't find anything to say. So he lay quiet. Scripta indicated the dead man's rifle. "An enemy weapon. Looks like an old French lever action .30–.30. You know how to work one?"

Butwell crawled to the dead man. He was scared. He felt as though he were making a moving target of himself. Some sharpshooter would appreciate that. His hands shook when he stripped the corpse of its bandoleer of bullets. Then he brought both gun and ammunition back to Scripta. "What now, Sergeant?"

Scripta never took his eyes off the village. "Between here and that pagoda, this ditch shallows out. To move along that, they'll have to expose themselves. If we catch movement, we call for mortar fire. That'll end their day."

Butwell was beginning to see the logic behind Scripta's thinking. "But why this ditch? Why not any other? There must be half a dozen of them out there."

The sergeant jerked a thumb at the dead enemy. "Him. He tells me a lot. He was a one-man scouting force. So it must mean a small party coming along. Something like about our size. If it was a big war party, the advance would have been a squad."

Butwell didn't like this. Everything depended on how this young kid happened to think. What was needed here was a trained tactician, not some child who figured survival like a cornered rat. "What about Moir and Vose, Sergeant?"

Scripta grunted. "After this piece of action, we'll call in a chopper for air evac. They'll fly out the wounded. And if you don't flatten yourself, you'll be one of them."

"You mean medics will fly in?"

The sergeant nodded, but he remained silent. His eyes

had caught movement. He waved Eagle-eye close. The Indian was still carrying the trench knife between his teeth. "Take that knife out of your mouth. You ain't Sitting Bull. Nobody's getting scalped."

Eagle-eye replaced the knife in its sheath. "What'cha want, Sarge?"

"Out there," the sergeant said. "Out along that ditch. In that open space. What'cha see?"

Butwell was also eager for a look. He scrambled alongside Eagle-eye. He was astonished at what he saw. A number of large-hatted figures were hurrying away from the village quite a distance off, a little hard to distinguish.

"Amazing," he mumbled to himself. "Absolutely amazing."

Things were happening just as this foxy kid had predicted. Then he felt a letdown. These were women. Big hats meant women. These were workers going to the rice paddies. Killing women wasn't their bag.

Scripta seemed to think otherwise. "Radio," he called. "Tell 'em to pull the plug. Maybe six rounds."

"God in heaven, no," Butwell yelled. "You're not going to gun down women!"

Sergeant Scripta ignored him. "On the line. Safeties off. Fire after first mortar impact."

There was a rattling as men on the firing line readied their M-16 rifles. From the distant perimeter came the faint thunk of .81-mm mortar shells being dropped into firing tubes. Butwell counted six distinct thunks.

"This is murder," Butwell yelled at Scripta.

The sergeant was busy. He turned to the riflemen sprawled along the lip of the ditch. "Ready on the line."

"No, no," Butwell pleaded. "Can't you see they're women?"

Scripta shoved him aside. He was studying his wrist-watch. After what seemed like an eternity of quiet, there was a boom. Then there was another and another as the mortar shells hit home. Riflemen opened up. Butwell found himself witness to a scene of slaughter. The row of women was shattered. The mortar strikes were right on target. The landscape erupted into a dirty cloud. Riflemen pumped a steady rain of fire into the upheaval.

Butwell was whimpering. "No, no, not women. No, no."

Scripta waved his hand. The line went silent. "Radio. Pass the word to perimeter, hold fire. We're moving forward for a look."

Leaping to his feet, he waved the men up. "Follow me."

They all scrambled upright and began a slow shuffle forward. Rifles at the ready, hunched over, quiet. Butwell followed along, angry and humiliated over what Scripta had brought about. "Sergeant," he called. "I'm going to report this. That's what I'm here for, to report the truth. To tell the facts as I see them."

Several bullets cracked overhead. That was enemy fire from the ditch. Scripta's squad took care of that. A blast now and then cut any resistance. As a final precaution, they laced the ditch with bullets. Then there was silence.

"Olephant's been hit," someone called along the line. He was one of their own riflemen. Scripta kept plodding forward. "Close in, close in," he called again and again.

Butwell was aghast. This was a being without mercy. No wonder the Vietcong hated Americans. Then they were at the scene of destruction.

"Radio," Scripta yelled. "Call in medical air evac. Tell 'em we got three wounded. None serious. No dead."

For the first time in a long while, the sergeant stood erect. He stretched. He had a grin on his face and appeared satisfied. "Good work, men," he called. "Nice job. We nailed every one of them. Now we can return to the perimeter."

Butwell was furious. This beast. This bloodthirsty teen-age killer. He was actually proud of his handiwork. "Scripta," he said. "You won't be grinning when you read the story I write."

The sergeant turned sober for a moment. He eyed the reporter critically. "You forgot to fire your weapon. Put that in your story, too."

"I will. And I'm proud to say I'm not a killer of women."

Scripta was standing over one of the dead bodies. A large pointed hat hid the face. A woman's pigtails could be seen sticking from beneath the headdress. Callously, Scripta put out a foot and flipped the hat aside.

A man!

The pigtails were fastened to the rim of the straw hat. Butwell could only gasp in surprise. His astonishment was made worse by Eagle-eye. "Twelve of 'em, Sarge. All dressed like women. Each armed with a rifle. Two of them carrying mortar tubes."

The Indian walked close to Scripta. He patted the sergeant fondly on the shoulder. "Nice going, ol' buddy. Outmanned and outgunned, we didn't lose a soldier. Not a single American life lost."

"Reporter," the sergeant said, "be sure to put *that* in your story."

Index

Abdel, Corporal, 26–37
Armstrong, Sergeant, 104
Asfaw, Colonel, 83–85

Baker, Lieutenant, 13–15
Baldwin, First Sergeant, 92–105
"Bed-check Charlie," German aircraft, 31, 37
Black market in Salerno, 17–25
Butwell, Corporal, combat reporter, 106–116

Cinel, Major, 83–85
Collins, Chaplain, 29–31, 33–37
Combat reporter teams, 80–88
Combat reporters
    Butwell, Corporal, 106–116
    Darling, Daniel, 5–15, 49, 53–55
    Hoops, Oliver, 69–79
    Murphy, Patrick, 7, 41–46
    Olcheskie, Howard, 7, 57–67

Stein, Herman, 7, 32–37
Sweeney, James B., 31
Van Vlack, Jan, 7, 17–25
Woodstock, Bruno, 81–91
Combat reporting
    casualty rate, 2, 7
    training and indoctrination, 5–10
Combat reports, 8–10, 11–15
Corns, Lieutenant, 60

Darling, Daniel, combat reporter, 5–15, 49, 53–55
de Gaulle, Charles, 49
Disappearance of Major General Laske, 47–55
Doyle, First Sergeant, 13–15
Du, Captain, 84–91

"Eagle-eye," 108–109, 110–111, 114, 116
Edgewood, Major, 17–25

82nd Airborne Division, 17
Elliott, Sergeant, 56
Exposing medical fraud, 26–37
Exposing a spy, 80–91
Extrasensory perception (ESP), 92–105

Faulkner, Captain, 26–34
1st Infantry Division, 59
"Flying Squads," 80–88
Forster, General, 42–46
French resistance, 47–55

German prisoners of war, 38–46
German troops, 47–55, 62–67
Grimes, Harry, 11–15
Grimes, Joe, 11–15

Hatami, Major, 83–85, 89–91
Hawke, Private, 38–46
Hitler, 1, 43, 47, 49, 52
Hoops, Oliver, combat reporter, 69–79
Hu, Colonel, 83–85, 89–91
Hunter, Lieutenant, 27–32

Infiltration of Korean forces, 80–91
Interrogation of German prisoners, 38–46

Japanese troops, 8–10, 11–15

Knuckles, General, 80
Korean warfare, 69–79, 80–91

"Lank," 71–79
Laske, Major General, 47–55
Levittre, Captain, 52–53
Lourdes, France, 35–36

MacArthur, General, 73, 76
McGee, Private, 100–102
Marshall, General, 2
Medical fraud, 26–37
Murphy, Patrick, combat reporter, 7, 41–46

96th Infantry Division, 11
9th Armored Division, 63
Nord, Colonel, 26–32
North Korean troops, 69–78, 80–88

Olcheskie, Howard, combat reporter, 7, 57–67
115th Infantry Division, 26
101st Airborne Division, 63
Opal, Corporal, 60–61, 63, 65–67

Patrol in Vietnam, 106–116
Patton, General, 26
Pergrin, First Sergeant, 60
Philadelphia, Pennsylvania, 89
Piquet, Father, 53–55

Quincy, Corporal, 92–105

Reporters, combat. *See* Combat reporters
Reports, combat, 8–10, 11–15
Republic of Korea (ROK) Capitol Division, 81
Russian roulette, 22–25

Salerno, Italy, 17
Schmidt, Captain, 39–46
Scripta, Sergeant, 106–116
Search and destroy mission, Vietnam, 97–103
7th Infantry Division, 11

Shik, Colonel, 83–85
Shirer, Mess Sergeant, 56–67
Song, General, 81–85, 90–91
Spy, exposure of, 80–91
Stein, Herman, combat reporter, 7, 32–37
Sweeney, James B., combat reporter, 31

10th Armored Division, 63
Teresa, Tony, 18–25
3rd Infantry Division, 32
378th Port Battalion, 38
Thunderbird Infantry Division, 47
Training and indoctrination for combat reporting, 5–10
Troueville, France, 47

12th Infantry Division, 92

U.S. prisoners of war, 8–10, 13–15, 69–79

Van Thieu, Colonel, 83–85
Van Vlack, Jan, combat reporter, 7, 17–25
Vietnam warfare, 92–105, 106–111

Woodstock, Bruno, combat reporter, 81–91
World War II, 5–15, 17–25, 26–37, 38–46, 47–55, 56–67

Zaphire, Sergeant, 56

About the Author

James B. Sweeney, a now retired Lieutenant Colonel of the
U.S. Air Force, spent twenty-five years as a combat reporter,
serving in the U.S. Merchant Service, the National Guard, the
Regular Army, the Air Force, and as a civilian with the Navy.
He covered stories in over twenty-three countries, interviewed
many notables over the years, and received a Bronze Star, four
Commendation medals, and six Combat Battle Star medals for
his combat reporting.

Mr. Sweeney, who has written numerous books and arti-
cles on the sea and underwater exploration, in this book hopes
to remedy the fact that, in his own words, "combat reporters
are the unsung heroes of warfare."